MAKING CHANGE

Teaching Artists and Their Role in Shaping a Better World

Eric Booth

BETTERYET PRESS

BY THE TENS OF THOUSANDS, *teaching artists in every country have poured their hearts and best creative energies into activating artistry throughout this world that is both beautiful and such a mess.*

My life and this book are dedicated to them.

©2023 Eric Booth
ISBN: 978-0-578-48279-8
Registered with U.S. Library of Congress, 2023

All income from sales of this book will be donated to ITAC—the International Teaching Artist Collaborative.

Praise for *Making Change*

"Teaching artists amplify the power of the arts; they widen the reach; they engage everyone; and they do that with beauty. You'll find out how in this inspiring book—and no one better than Eric Booth to share these stories."
—CLIVE GILLINSON, *Executive and Artistic Director, Carnegie Hall*

"*Making Change* is absolutely riveting! I hope many read this beautifully crafted work and realise how art can reimagine the world into a kinder, more peaceful and inclusive one!"—SANGEETA ISVARIN, *Founder, Wind Dancers Trust; Co-Founder, Katradi Method: Arts for Conflict Resolution, India*

"What is a teaching artist? The concept is subtle, and unfamiliar to many. Eric Booth to the rescue, with his uncanny ability to describe nuance with the precision of a laser beam. Teaching artists worldwide be grateful for this profoundly useful and provocative book—and readers new to the subject will find themselves fascinated and inspired by these stories from the exuberant front lines of teaching artistry."—JAMIE BERNSTEIN, *Author,* Famous Father Girl; *Filmmaker,* Crescendo: The Power of Music

"Artistry in the deepest sense, as Eric Booth grasps it, has the power to move the human project forward. Every parent, leader, teacher, and therapist would benefit from the clarity of the insights and practical know-how contained in this succinct but powerful manifesto." —JOHN ZWEIG, *Chairman, Neuro-Insight; Director, Foundation for Art and Healing*

"Eric Booth expands our sense of what's possible when we activate the innate sense of curiosity, playfulness, and creativity within us all. At this historical moment when many are re-imagining what teaching and learning could be, Eric's hard-earned wisdom serves as a beacon for a brighter, creatively rich future." —STU WARSHAWER, *CEO, ArtistYear*

"This book addresses the need to rethink the role of artists in society and offers an account of how artists can be healers, educators, and advocate. Eric Booth shows us that if we can find creative ways to use artists for social change, we can find new solutions to making the world a better place."
—CARLA DIRLIKOV CANALES, *2022–23 Fellow, Harvard Kennedy School Center for Public Leadership Social Innovation + Change Initiative*

"The international Teaching Artist community has been an incredibly useful resource for organizations around the world. It has shone a light along our path as we work to make music make a difference."
—ELIZABETH NJOROGE, *Founder of The Art of Music Foundation, Nairobi*

Praise for other books by Eric Booth:

The Everyday Work of Art

"This book takes an insightful look at the wonder with which we can approach our lives and reminds us of the importance of perceiving the extraordinary in the ordinary."—YO-YO MA, *musician*

"This book is important, taking us in a direction we've forgotten or ignored. It reminds us of the necessity of the arts for the growth and health of the human spirit."—MADELEINE L'ENGLE, *author*

The Music Teaching Artist's Bible

"Bless Eric Booth for showing us how to better do our job. And bless this book for showing us musicians how we can bring our audiences more deeply inside the music in practical, fun, and satisfying ways."
—BOBBY MCFERRIN, *musician*

"This is the most anticipated book in the performing arts world—by artists who want to teach as well as they play, by concert presenters and educators dying to engage artists who know how to communicate, and by audiences, young and old alike, ready to be transformed by artists who have the desire to…simply change lives. The 'bible' is finally here … and the master teacher artist wrote it!"—KENNETH C. FISCHER, *President, University Musical Society, University of Michigan*

"This is a timely and very useful book. The role of the teaching artist is growing in the world. Booth's book shows how to do it well and affirms the importance of this burgeoning profession."—MARIN ALSOP, *conductor*

Playing for Their Lives

"*Playing for Their Lives* brings us the news that not only is it possible to change the lives of children through music … it's already happening on a worldwide scale. This book is an important call to action for people everywhere."
—QUINCY JONES, *music producer*

"Anyone looking for evidence of the transformative power of the arts should read this important book."—DANIEL H. PINK, *author*

"*Playing for Their Lives* affirms the power of music to change lives and communities. This is a book every orchestra lover must read, but also every community organizer, every school board member, and every citizen artist who is ready to change the world."—JOSHUA BELL, *violinist*

Contents

Introduction 7

Part One:
Activating Artistry 11

What's the Purpose of Teaching Artistry? 14

What Can Teaching Artistry Actually Do? 19

What Does the Work of Teaching Artistry Actually Look Like? 24

A Short History of the Field of Teaching Artistry 28

Who Becomes a Teaching Artist? And Why? 31

What's the Difference between a Teaching Artist and an Arts Teacher? 35

Some Examples of Teaching Artistry in Action 40

The Fundamentals of Teaching Artistry 45

Why Doesn't Everyone Everywhere Know about Teaching Artistry? 48

Imagining What's Possible 50

What We Could Do with a Big Investment 55

Part Two:
Teaching Artist Tools and Purposes 61

The Tools of Teaching Artistry 63

Routines and Rituals that Support
Teaching Artist Practice 77

At the Intersection of Teaching
Artistry and Performance 81

The Purpose Threads 85

Beyond a Specific Purpose 101

Acknowledgements 105
About the Author 105
Endnotes 107
Other Books on Teaching Artistry 109
Index 109

Introduction

IN THE ROHINGYA REFUGEE CAMP in Bangladesh, tensions were running high between Bangladeshis and Rohingya refugees. The Artolution[1] program brought in teaching artists who led a project in the joint creation, by refugees and Bangladeshis working together, of a series of giant, colorful murals throughout the community that vividly depicted health concerns shared by all participants. Tensions lessened markedly, and the local government changed policies in response to the health concerns.

*

THE SING SING CORRECTIONAL FACILITY is a maximum-security prison in New York State that houses 1,400 convicted men, most serving long-term sentences. Every week, a few dozen of them—currently thirty-five, few of whom had played a musical instrument before—gather in a room and make music for hours, led by teaching artists from Carnegie Hall. The program has a long waiting list. Within months of beginning, they were playing and singing together; within a year, they were performing original compositions in front of a packed house of other men at the facility. Curriculum varies; teaching artists sometimes dedicate an entire year to the study of one composer, guiding composition in that style (one year was dedicated to Duke Ellington's Sacred Music, another to women in music, another to Afrofuturism). One member of the group performed an evening of his music at Carnegie Hall on the day of his release. None of those in the program have "re-offended" after their incarceration.

*

GOTHENBURG, SWEDEN, an old and robust port city on the North Sea, has become a major endpoint in the journeys of refugees from a host of countries in turmoil—Afghanistan, Syria, Albania, Somalia and many more. Some of these refugees are children and teenagers who arrived alone, without their families, after terrifying journeys of uncertainty and danger. Seven years ago, teaching artists at a community music for social change program began giving these young people instruments and group lessons (and, often, food and shelter); today, they are accomplished members of The Dream Orchestra,[2] a performing and touring ensemble that participates fully in Gothenburg life. The orchestra became their family, and the music became their lifeline.

*

LIKE SO MANY coastal cities, São José, Santa Catarina, Brazil, is increasingly battered by climate change. Many citizens feel hopeless, even disconnected, because of the rising crisis. The School of the (Im)Possible (devised by local teaching artists at Platô Cultural[3]) worked with classes of nine-year-olds for ten weeks in school, making them secret agents in touch with a climate scientist living in 2072, who invited them to join an (im)possible mission: "to re-write the future with sustainable solutions." In the all-absorbing mystery improvisation, the teaching artist guide helped them gather clues, study the local environment, take careful notes and solve challenges, eventually to write their own books about what's going on and what they want to do about it. In a culminating event at the school, they confronted their parents (who don't usually attend school events) and local leaders with hard questions about what the grown-ups were going to do about these challenges. The kids became the environmental educators and activists of São José. The mayor ordered The School of the (Im)Possible to spread to schools across the city; it has also been adopted in two schools in Scotland.

*

FOUR STORIES among thousands in which engaging in the arts provided solutions to the world's most intractable challenges. This book introduces the workforce of artists, called teaching artists, who do this work. With joy.

Part One:
Activating Artistry

Everyone brims with artistry.

Call it what you will, deny it if you like—we all have it. We use it here, there and everywhere we make things we care about. Like cooking a special meal. Or getting into a great conversation. Or adding final touches to an important presentation. Or making up a story for a child—or making up a story as a child. Of course, there is artistry in symphonies and sculpture, and there is an artistry to bricklaying and pie-making. There are books about the art of tennis and the art of motorcycle maintenance. We even use the term "medical arts."

So what? Why does artistry matter a lick in the complex, speedy, pragmatic world we inhabit? Slow down and read on—you will recognize this ancient, underutilized power tool that not only creates beauty but also creates change. This book honors the arts workers who know how to use that tool, who delight in activating its use, and who do so, often quietly but with remarkable effectiveness, around the world.

Does "artistry" sound effete or elitist? If so, you might want to talk to a great carpenter, or a great surgeon, nurse, athlete, therapist, teacher, chef, gardener or waiter. Anyone who gets absorbed and creatively engaged in their work can tell you where artistry lives in their success. Artistry makes the difference between competence and excellence; between good enough and beautiful. Maybe you prefer a different word, like creativity, or flow experience, or innovative capacity—functionally, they mean pretty much the same thing. Whatever you want to call it, life, work, love, and just about everything that matters goes better when we are using it. Some animals show signs of having artistry—I'm looking at you, bowerbirds—but theirs is modest compared with human artistry.

Artistry isn't effete or elitist; it is strong, muscular stuff. It's not reserved for special people who became "artists" through rigorous, years-long study and now do wonderful things in artistic disciplines like paints and dance and music and acting. It's a universal human capacity and an essential shaper of human progress. We all know about the debut evidence of art in those cave paintings created 30,000 years ago, or the simple bone flutes of 33,000 BCE. But artistry was a driving force in human development many hundreds of thousands of years before those visual and musical arts started their long journeys. It drove creative innovations in hunting, in toolmaking, in shelter-making, in language development and then storytelling, probably in mate selection, in all kinds of experimentation since our earliest human days.

In our contemporary world, the power of artistry for social development is still at work in the evolving worldwide field known as "arts for social impact" or "arts for social change." Maybe you've heard one of these phrases and thought that it was just a marketing catchphrase for arts organizations trying to appear more relevant. Maybe it just sounded like wishful thinking.

Or maybe you know that arts for social impact is, indeed, a potent and growing movement across the world that has proven its effectiveness and transformational potential—but you wonder, who are the professionals who actually *do this work?*

In either case, you're reading the right book.

THERE IS AN ENTIRE PROFESSION dedicated to activating people's artistry for a range of purposes. These professionals know how to awaken artistry. They know how to develop it. They know how to guide it toward positive results, results that matter.

There are several names for this workforce that knows how to tap and guide the power of human artistry. In some cultures, these skilled workers are called community artists or participatory artists; in others, social practice artists or citizen artists or artist-educators. In places where artists work in communities all the time, they are simply called artists.

In this book, we will call them teaching artists. The workforce doesn't quibble about nomenclature (we did for a time, but that's largely outgrown); we care about the pleasures and powers of our work to make the world a better place.

You can find teaching artists, or whatever they are called locally, in every country. They usually work without fanfare and are always underpaid for the amount of good they produce. They work in community centers, in schools, and in art places like museums and performance halls; you'll find some in hospitals, businesses, government agencies, and prisons. You can probably find them in every city and town, if you take the time to look.

What's the purpose of teaching artistry?

WHEN ACTIVATING PEOPLE'S innate artistry, teaching artists can guide that energy toward many goals. In Part Two of this book, I will give you a tour of the seven major goals teaching artists are hired to deliver. Here is a preview. They are hired...

1. To develop important personal or social capacities.

Creative youth development programs around the world build leadership skills and increase life options for young people in stressful situations and historically-underserved communities. Creative aging, involving older people in artistic projects, has proven to have dramatically positive, life-extending (and cost-saving) impact. This sector provides the most active expansion of teaching artist employment in the U.S.

2. To enhance the life of communities.

There is a long history of using collective artmaking—murals, choruses, parades (hello, Mardi Gras) and more—to celebrate the community, to handle serious blows and to address pressing issues. Schools, workplaces and interest groups are communities too.

3. To impact political and social movements.

Activist artists have long been influential in moving the public toward greater commitment for or against powerful issues. Sometimes teaching artists are employed to provide their distinctive difference. For example, ITAC (International Teaching Artist Collaborative[4]) and other non-governmental organizations (NGOs) commission teaching artists around the world to activate communities through creative projects that address the climate crisis. Social justice is embedded in a teaching artist's worldview—even in projects without stated goals of changing cultural and political realities—because all teaching artist work embodies egalitarian fairness. The working environments they create model the communities they strive to bring into the world. Communities of active respect and kind appreciation—communities of radical welcome.

4. To achieve goals important to non-arts institutions.

Organizations and agencies are catching on to the fact that teaching artists can help them accomplish things they struggle with: more innovation in corporations, better diagnoses in hospitals, better communication in government agencies, stronger public engagement in community development, safer streets, more peaceful prisons, better nutrition, less litter—on and on. No one can count how many lives have been saved in the AIDS/HIV pandemic by the adoption of safer sex practices taught through theater for social development programs in African communities. Want to move faster toward the United Nations' Sustainable Development Goals?[5] Invest in teaching artists. They know how to develop the Inner Development Goals[6] that are essential to achieving those Sustainable Development Goals.

5. To deepen the development of artmaking skills.

Artist training programs, conservatories and university arts departments increasingly recognize that the skills of teaching artistry expand the understandings and careers of emerging artists, and they make them more employable too.

6. To boost the learning of non-arts subjects.

Schools (and professional development programs) use arts-integrated projects to raise academic achievement and learner engagement, even in STEM subjects (science, technology, engineering and math), becoming STEAM programs by adding the arts.

7. To enrich encounters with art works.

Museums and performing arts companies rely on teaching artists to deepen the experiences of current audiences, to broaden their reach and excite currently-disengaged audiences and to develop future audiences.

THAT RANGE OF GOALS shows the wide embrace that teaching artistry brings to art. There's been a long debate in the U.S. and other Western cultures about the purpose of art: "art for art's sake" versus "art for practical purposes." One camp celebrates the power of art to enrich life in ways nothing else can or ever has; Walter Benjamin[7] described this as "a theology of art." These devoted "people of the arts" want to protect that force from getting diluted or polluted by practical application, creating safe havens and ever-higher prices. The other camp recognizes the distinctive, sometimes unique, potential of art to create positive change in the world—an equally estimable cause, since the world could do with some improvement. "Art for art's sake" is about the *intrinsic* enrichment that experiencing or making art brings to our lives and cultures. "Art for positive change" is about the many benefits that the arts can be instrumental in producing.

For a long time, these two positions were opposed and entrenched, arguing their respective merits in the court of public perception and to prospective funders. Funders care about both, which is why you see both in the employment goals listed above, but they have cared about art for art's sake a whole lot more. That perspective has had far more power, more money and more status—no wonder we refer to the "high arts" and build glorious temples for them. Walk into an empty concert hall and you feel the aura, a kind of sanctity by design. This prestige shows the embedded vertical hierarchy in most Western and Western-influenced cultures, earning them their "elitist" reputation at the top of the funding and status ladder. Art in the practical and everyday world is omnipresent, but doesn't get a capital "A" or the temples or the hefty funding.

IS THIS REALLY an either-or, high-low, *Art-vs.-art conundrum?*

Not according to a major research report from The Wallace Foundation in 2005. *Gifts of the Muse: Reframing the Debate about the Benefits of the Arts*[8] recognized that, obviously, both kinds of impact are valuable; society wants and needs both. Humans have always wanted and needed both. The report clarified the relationship between the two kinds of impact, concluding that you can only get the instrumental benefits if you go through the gateway of the intrinsic. In other words, humans have to experience artistry personally, in some way, in order to open the door for all those other more practical (and more measurable) benefits the arts can bring. Nobody buys an opera ticket to improve the economic viability of their downtown. But if enough people are having rewarding artistic experiences in the opera house, they come back with friends, have dinner at a local restaurant, and support the downtown economy. No student tries to capture the drama of a scene about Frederick Douglass meeting Abraham Lincoln in order to improve their midterm test score, but if they pour their heart into the significance of that encounter and try to capture its drama in a scene they write, their test scores in American History go up. There is no shortcut; you can't just skip to the practical payoffs of the arts without activating (and enjoying) the messier and less-conveniently measurable business of personal artistry.

> [Y]ou can only get the instrumental benefits if you go through the gateway of the intrinsic.

This is where teaching artists come in. They can activate the artistry in pretty much anyone, opening up an entire range of possible benefits, both instrumental and intrinsic—from better health outcomes in the senior living center to a deeper experience of Brahms' Second Symphony.

The advice of the great 20th-century physicist David Bohm has been a guideline for my life: any time you see seeming opposites, look for the greater truth that contains them both. For me and for other teaching artists, the deeper truth underneath the push-pull of art for art's sake versus art for social impact is art for many sakes. Both intentions spring from the same source, and our positive future requires tapping that deeper source. That's what teaching artists do.

What can teaching artistry actually do?

IN THE LATE 1990S, BOGOTA, *Colombia had horrifically high traffic fatality rates. The traffic police were corrupt and no attempted solution made any difference.* Mayor Antanas Mockus fired all the cops, offering to rehire them if they trained as mimes. The mime-trained, mime-costumed cops took to the streets, mocking bad drivers, cheering safe drivers and comically dramatizing the realities of dealing with traffic. There was a 50% drop in traffic deaths, significantly reduced gridlock and a lasting shift in the traffic culture of the city.

IN THE EARLY YEARS of teaching artistry in the U.S., we worked mostly in schools. Our goal was to empower students to have relevant, engaging artistic experiences. We were focusing on art for art's sake, but our classroom teacher partners told us they noticed additional benefits from our work. Students became better learners in other subjects. Teamwork improved in classrooms, which then became happier communities. Kids were more motivated to read. Disciplinary referrals declined.

As this original school-based work has matured in the U.S., we've seen additional benefits. Those practical outcomes may be hard to strategically predict, and even harder to measure, but it's clear that the ripple effect is reliable and real. When working in schools, teaching artists are disproportionately impactful for the amount of time we spend with kids—not much time and a whole lot of benefit. (By the way, give us more time and we can accomplish a whole lot more. And, usually, the most transformative impact is felt by the students who struggle hardest to succeed

[W]hen teaching artists activate the artistry of young people, positive outcomes arise.

within standard school practices.) Over and over, we see that when teaching artists activate the artistry of young people, positive outcomes arise. (When anyone activates the artistry of young people, positive outcomes arise—teaching artists just happen to be specialists at it.)

This ripple effect applies to teachers and whole schools too. Teachers feel rejuvenated and use a greater range of creative teaching tools; schools become more vibrant communities; parents get more involved. Such outcomes are particularly dramatic in "arts-infused" schools, and schools that develop "arts-rich,"[9] "Turnaround Arts"[10] and "Artful Learning"[11] programs to tap the transformative power of activated artistry.

These days, teaching artistry's reach has grown far beyond schools. Around the world, many hundreds of arts for social change programs use teaching artists outside of school hours to guide hundreds of thousands of young people living communities of poverty or in stressful conditions toward lives with more options and agency. Young people in detention in Berkshire County, Massachusetts are released early if they stay in a Shakespeare workshop taught by Shakespeare & Company[12] teaching artists, because the impact on them is so positive. No kids join the active gangs in Whangarei, New Zealand, if they join the teaching artist-led youth orchestra[13] instead.

These positive impacts are felt by everybody, not just young people. Working in prisons, teaching artists help people create meaning and connection even in settings of tension and alienation. Working in hospitals, they can serve similar purposes, even creating better health outcomes. Working in community and social service centers, they can make all the difference in people's wellbeing.

TEACHING ARTISTRY'S IMPACT can be especially profound in refugee camps and settlement communities. Teaching artists help create a sense of home where people desperately need one. Witness the successes of the Dream Orchestra[14] in Sweden and El Sistema Greece[15] in Athens, or the beautiful work of Sounds of Change,[16] which trains musicians to bring joy to challenging circumstances around the world. Even in such volatile conditions, teaching artists alleviate personal and collective trauma, ease political and racial tensions and help develop bonds of powerful connection between people who have lost such bonds. Every refugee and resettlement community in the world should have teaching-artists-in-residence.

In the field of creative aging, the fastest-growing sector of teaching artistry in the U.S., this work has also proven to make a difference: reducing prescription drug intake and length of hospital stays, improving quality of life and adding good years of longevity, uplifting staff morale, improving employee retention rates—and resulting in significant savings for those institutions and governments. It can ease the suffering of people with dementia. For people of all ages, it can reduce depression and increase hopefulness; in some countries (like those in the U.K.), doctors write prescriptions to work with teaching artists instead of taking more medication.

TEACHING ARTISTS can even sharpen the diagnostic accuracy of medical doctors: in the U.S., there are over twenty partnerships between medical schools and art museums, wherein teaching artists work with medical students to open up new ways of perceiving works of art—ways that transfer to perceiving and diagnosing maladies more accurately. Yes, teaching artists save lives, literally.

Government agencies are discovering that teaching artists can make them more effective. In fact, over a dozen cities in the U.S. (including the two largest) place teaching artists in different departments because their creative engagement skills disrupt assumptions, energize staff and often generate new outcomes. Businesses, too, are discovering that teaching artists can help employees become more creative. The most common assignment I was hired to deliver in businesses was "more creativity, but no art, please." They fear the emotional touchy-feely stickiness they associate with art. "Fine, I can do that," I assure them. And then I do what teaching artists do, without using arts vocabulary or artsy media. Often, business participants don't even know that artistry is in play, even though it always is. I've worked with high-tech metallurgical engineers, leaders in a major hospital's thoracic care division, the marketing department of an Ivy League university, Federal Express' Board of Directors, a seminary faculty and the leadership development programs of three cities. Each time, I was able to deliver the results the organization wanted.

Teaching artists can make celebrations more joyful, rituals more meaningful and public events more impactful. Almost anywhere they show up, they help people make things more beautiful. They provide access to wonder in situations and people who need it; scientists have increasingly found that experiencing wonder provides significant physical and psychological benefits to individuals and groups.

PERHAPS MOST URGENT OF ALL, teaching artists can make a crucial contribution to climate crisis response—a contribution that is more effective than the most well-intentioned artwork can be. Many artists, of course, care about the environment; hundreds make heartfelt works of art to communicate their concern. These artworks can be beautiful and moving contributions to the cause. But do they have the social impact that our code-red crisis needs? For example, in a recent project, hundreds of thousands of dollars were spent to make a gorgeous five-camera film of a renowned musician playing a new composition about climate change on a Steinway concert grand piano, placed on an acoustically perfect raft that floated in front of a calving Arctic glacier. Some of the people who see that film will be impressed and touched. But has it significantly changed one single person's understanding or actions?

For a sliver of that budget, a teaching artist can go into a community affected by climate change and creatively engage people to awaken latent commitment that overcomes apathy and hopelessness. Minds, hearts, understandings change, a sense of personal agency arises, and they take action that can lead to real policy change. This is exactly what the crisis requires, and teaching artistry can deliver it.

Does it sound to you like this workforce can do anything? If so, you're pretty close to the truth. I bet my money on them. But as things stand now, not enough people are placing their money on teaching artists for them to realize their potential. Their talents and skills are powerful but under-tapped. The broader public, for the most part, doesn't know or see what they do. There are even many people in the arts who don't know about teaching artists. Few funders invest in developing this workforce. There aren't many train-

> Teaching artistry is the sleeping giant of social change.

❖

ing pathways available to bring young talent into the field, and there are few career pathways to move up. The field doesn't have much infrastructure that helps them gain visibility (although the International Teaching Artist Collaborative, ITAC, is making headway). This could change—is ripe to change—if funders invest in developing and supporting the teaching artist workforce. Teaching artistry is the sleeping giant of social change.

What Does the Work of Teaching Artistry Actually Look Like?

ARTISTS KNOW AND CAN DO important things—essential things. They have a nuanced understanding about the relationship between parts and wholes. They see time, reality and inevitability as malleable raw materials with which to shape new worlds. They can imagine the world as if it were otherwise. They can make a coherent world that eloquently holds what they know and care about. They can make meaning that others can then grasp as their own.

Teachers know and can do equally essential things. They know that learning is the way humans stay alive and grow. They can guide others to follow intrinsic curiosity, to explore the unfamiliar, to expand the scope and depth of their explorations. They can midwife evolving meanings and shape evolving understandings.

Teaching artists know and can do an additional thing that melds the essential elements of each vocation: they know how to draw others into environments of change and possibility. They can stir and activate the artistic impulse in others and then guide it, using both what artists know and what teachers know. Crucially, they are able to cultivate individual and social imagination. And right now, social imagination is what the world most desperately needs.

TEACHING ARTISTS' work looks different across projects and cultural settings, but some features always appear. Whether the work is happening in a workshop room at Carnegie Hall or inside a red earth circle in a Tanzanian village, teaching artists will design step-by-step activities that guide people who aren't "artists" into creative work. The activities are always highly engaging and fun (I call it "the ruthless use of fun"); even people who "don't much like the arts" find themselves fully invested, using artistic materials and processes they would have avoided an hour earlier. Teaching artists guide people to use their imagination and make stuff they care about—stuff that is personally relevant, challenging in just the right ways, emotionally connected and satisfying to complete. They usually (but not always) guide a group to work both individually and together. They bring people to full attention and into flow experiences. Participants find pleasure in reflecting on their creative processes. The burst of energy that comes with creating can be skillfully shepherded, by a teaching artist, toward social impact goals that matter.

Allow me a slight digression that helps me explain what it is that teaching artists do. Most of Western culture defines Art by its nouns—its buildings, its ballades and its ballets. The U.S., in particular, is the noun-centric hub of the known universe, so Art is made of things. However, teaching artists are masters of the *verbs* of art—the things artists do to make those artworks. They are the same verbs all people use when they make things they care about, in any medium, when their artistry kicks in. Sure, the things made in artistic media—the paintings and modern dances, the art "nouns"—can be valuable and important, often beautiful, even magnificent sometimes. But the power lies in the verbs. I wrote a book about that, *The Everyday Work of Art*.

Works of art are tombstones that mark locations where significant acts of aliveness once took place. They await fresh verbs to bring them back to life. That Picasso on the wall, that Shostakovich in the concert hall, are decorations until the verbs of art awaken our hunger for more aliveness, more pleasure, more meaning, more of some unnamable yearning in us. That yearning impels us to burrow into those nouns by Picasso and Shostakovich in a different way and discover things that matter to us. When we make a personally relevant connection, we bring them back to life.

The verbs that create those masterful nouns are the same verbs that we apply to any medium to make things we care about. The kinds of attention, questioning and intuitive judgment of better and worse that thrive in artistry apply to both ballet and baking. The brainstorming and choice-making, the adding and subtracting, used in music are naturally tapped in gardening and fundraising. Creative problem-solving in producing a play shares more than you might expect with creative problem-solving in the Emergency Department of Mt. Sinai Hospital, or in a neighborhood where residents are organizing to make a playground. I know this firsthand; I have worked in all those settings, and in many others. That Federal Express leadership program I mentioned earlier learned more from studying how section leaders in the Memphis Symphony communicate with their section mates than they learned from a hundred-page instruction manual.

TEACHING ARTISTS ARE in the yearning business. When artistry is activated, people yearn to "make connections," both in discovering meaning in an artwork and in expressing themselves in arts or non-arts media. Look at the idiom—make a connection. It's a creative act, the atomic level of creativity. We do it all the time. It's a verb, after all.

Teaching Artists are in the yearning business

In a world wherein artificial intelligence programs can, in minutes, "produce" one hundred novels and "paint" fifty paintings that closely resemble the work of recognized masters—some of them remarkably good—our historic human relationship to the nouns of art gets unsettled. The creative intelligence skills, the verbs, in which teaching artists traffic grow more important in an AI world. The empathy, deftness and intuition that teaching artists bring to activating imagination and artistry in others and guiding them toward creative goals are not effete enrichments on the periphery of a healthy culture. They are a lifeline in a changing world.

There is one other thing. One essential thing about the way human artistry works. Something happens in us when we create something we care about—something reliable, powerful and mysterious. When we pour our artistry into a project, even one as small as making a personal connection, we experience a burst of creative satisfaction when we succeed. This moment is usually quiet, and may be so small we barely notice it, but the pleasure we experience is real. Creative success gives birth to a pop of energy toward further creation. A next idea or project. A follow-up or extension. A new question or curiosity. I call it "the bounce." Defying the first law of thermodynamics, a completion generates a spark of new energy. Creation, like love, is the rare human experience that generates more energy than it requires. It's got a bounce in its step.

Teaching artists use this bounce for the step-by-step design of activities that lead people to accomplishments beyond what they expect or even dream possible. In a few hours, with progressive bounces from creative satisfaction at each step, you can go from being an uncertain participant looking at an outdoor wall to a committed community advocate, standing proudly in front of a stunning mural that captures the aspirations of your neighborhood. In a few weeks, a town of hopeless victims of climate change can become a town of engaged citizens demanding local regulatory reform.

A Short History of the Field of Teaching Artistry

THERE HAVE ALWAYS BEEN artists who create art not only for self-expression or income but also to meet communities' essential needs. Artists of the Paleolithic Era did not paint animals on cave walls to wallow in the satisfaction of artistic creation or to earn tips from weekend touring groups; they painted to communicate something essential about hunting and perhaps to influence the spiritual forces that provided food. They were serving their community. Ever since, there have always been some artists who go beyond simply making artworks (granted, that is not so simple to do) to engage directly with community members for purposes other than art-for-art's-sake. In the U.S., community artists' stature rose when the 10,000-plus artists hired by the New Deal's Works Progress Administration (WPA, part of the 1935–1943 Federal Art Project) were celebrated for helping to lift the nation out of the Great Depression with their plays, dances, books, music and over 150,000 works of public visual art. In 1950, the organization Young Audiences began bringing artists into schools.

But teaching artistry as a distinct field, and later as a profession, began in the 1970s. In the U.S., it began with students. Common lore places the beginning at New York City's Lincoln Center, then the new "largest performing arts center in the world." Lincoln Center leaders began to explore ways they could more effectively engage the hundred-thousand students who walked across their plaza annually to see performances. Mark Schubart, the founder of Lincoln Center Institute, used to tell the story of walking by a line of kids waiting to enter the Metropolitan Opera and asking one boy what he was about to see. The boy's answer, with a dismissive shrug: "How should I know? It's just a field trip." Determined to do better than that, Schubart gathered a team of smart, experienced artists who had worked in schools. That group pulled together their own understandings and savvy from their previous project, and, inspired by the Institute's Philosopher-in-Residence Maxine Greene, started a new version of "aesthetic education." Essentially, this was the birth of teaching artistry as a field.

Teaching artistry as a U.S. profession got a boost in the 1980s, for a painful reason: federal cutbacks in arts education resulted in thousands of school arts teachers losing their jobs. Arts organizations hired teaching artists to go into schools to try to fill the gap, so that a generation would not grow up without a relationship to the arts. High arts organizations like symphony orchestras, ballet companies, theaters, art museums and their funders worried about future audiences, and time has proven those fears correct. Compared to the size of the problem, the investment in arts teachers and teaching artists has been far too small.

THE TEACHING ARTIST FIELD has steadily evolved. Teaching artists in schools became better partners in helping classroom teachers achieve their goals, training them to bring more creativity into their work; they have joined non-arts teachers in arts-integrated curricula in various subject areas. Many school residencies gradually grew longer (and sometimes shorter during economic downturns), allowing them to learn how to target various learning goals and assess the impact of their work. As the field grew, teaching artists got hired for projects outside of schools. Those thousands of artists who had already been working in neighborhoods and communities deepened and expanded their work. Artists who worked as "community artists" came to recognize their affinity with "teaching artists," and vice versa. In the U.S. and the U.K., projects arose to provide some infrastructure for the emerging field—the Teaching Artist Guild[17] in the U.S.; the ArtWorks Alliance[18] in the U.K. (The field has a vital life in the U.K., where it is called participatory artistry.)

With the birth of the International Teaching Artist Conferences in 2012 (which became the year-round International Teaching Artist Collaborative in 2018), isolated teaching artists around the world came to recognize that teaching artistry is a global field. The Academy for Impact through Music[19] now leads a training Fellowship with teaching artists from four continents. There are different strengths, titles, specific practices and employment patterns in different countries, but they share much more. They share a common core identity. The etymology of *identity* means *the same*. Organizational hubs are starting to gather in more countries and regions. A tipping point to global recognition is approaching.

Who Becomes a Teaching Artist? And Why?

TEACHING ARTISTS are practicing artists who yearn to do more than make works of art. It's great to make and share works of art—that's why people still get into the arts, even though everyone knows the career prospects are dicey. Many beginners have heard this grizzled advice—if you can bring yourself to do anything else, do that!—and don't listen. Making artworks is satisfying and fulfilling; it feels like who we are.

That's true for teaching artists too. But we have discovered that we want more. We love to make those nouns and to discover the pleasures and purposes of our own artistry, *and* we want to prepare students and audiences to successfully use the verbs of art to discover the beauty and importance that artworks contain. And we want lots of people—everyone, not just those attending artworks or trained to be artists—to be able to do this. And we want to engage the universal verbs of art to create positive change in the world. That's a lot of "ands"; teaching artists are ambitious.

You can't spot a teaching artist outside of our work. We might "look like artists" (whatever that means) or not. Some of us are shy and quiet; some are extraverted. We are younger and older. We are racially diverse, although the older set in the U.S., U.K. and Europe is pretty white while the younger set everywhere is more racially and ethnically mixed. We believe that diversity is an asset, that multiple perspectives make for richer creative results. We are all underpaid, and almost all juggle careers that include income from artmaking, teaching artistry, and often other things too. We tend to be entrepreneurial, partly by nature and mostly by necessity. We love to hang out with and work with other teaching artists and don't get to do it enough. Sometimes, teaching artists have to leave the field because it doesn't provide ways for them to earn more, even as their expertise grows. There is evidence that the Covid pandemic hit U.S. teaching artists harder than any other sector of the arts industries.

Teaching artistry is not a kitbag of handy educational tricks that an artist carries around to apply when circumstances invite. Teaching artistry is a worldview, an expansion of the artist's view. It includes fascination with the innate artistry in all people and excitement to discover what all people can create—from making connections inside artworks to making creative solutions for social problems.

Arts disciplines prioritize one set of criteria for excellence, with universities, professional associations and experts protecting (and enforcing) those inherited standards. As artists, teaching artists were trained to one definition of excellence; as teaching artists, they discover more. They still revere the excellence they learned in their arts discipline, but they also see other kinds of worthy accomplishments that deserve recognition and celebration—e.g., excellent resourcefulness, excellent social impact, excellence in cultural integrity.[20] These may not always meet the high arts' standards of excellence, but they are so remarkable in other ways that teaching artists honor them within a wider palette of excellence, one aligned with how humans have always lived and excelled.

Teaching artists are interested in people who are different from us, and especially curious about the creative ideas of young people, old people, people with different backgrounds, people with disabilities and people without a background in "the arts." We encourage the flair in all people we meet and then delight in the surprises we encounter. My own personal everyday curiosities tend to notice unusual uses of words, flashes of theatrical panache and small, quiet acts of kindness. I am at least as likely to discover these things in a shanty town as in an upscale shopping mall. What do you tend to notice about the artistry of others?

MOST PEOPLE WHO COME UPON a group of teenagers hanging out, who seem disengaged or discouraged, either don't see them or avoid them. An artist sees that group of kids and feels compassion. A teaching artist sees that group and can barely contain the impulse to invite them into an activity that would catch their interest. They want to engage with those kids to provide the pleasures and positives they know how to incite.

Some years ago, I was hired to lead a group of high school teachers in an after-school workshop about increasing creativity in their teaching. I remember walking up to the school building. It wasn't welcoming: as big as a government agency and every bit as imaginative in its design.

Three teenage friends were hanging out by a wall beside the entry stairs. These young men didn't exactly radiate trouble, but they were clearly the tough guys, the cool guys, who were about to exchange snide comments about the old dude heading into the school. I walked over to them. "Can you help me? I have to check in at the principal's office, but I'd like to get a sense of the school before I meet her. Can you tell me a way to get to her office, with a route that would take me by the most interesting stuff in the school?"

In two seconds, their snarky attitude was set aside, because—I'd guessed right—the unexpected challenge caught their interest. And this was a subject they really knew about. They started discussing options, brainstorming, teasing one another about their suggestions. There was a mention of the girl's locker room. One asked me what I was there for; he was refining the quality of the plan and wanted to make sure they made choices that were best for my purposes. After a full minute, they described their chosen map for me, all three of them talking, correcting one

How a teaching artist sees the world: brimming with potential.

another's directions with an occasional "you idiot" and describing the sights I would see. With brief thanks, I headed up the stairs and heard them continue to laughingly insult one another as they talked about the school's best and worst features. The playful genuineness of their exchange was definitely not "cool."

It's right there under the surface, much of the time, maybe most of the time, in all of us: the eagerness to take what we know and care about and to make something new and interesting with it. Even to make something useful for an uncool stranger. That's how a teaching artist sees the world, brimming with potential.

What's the Difference between a Teaching Artist and an Arts Teacher?

I AM OFTEN ASKED to draw this distinction, and it's a subtle one. The difference isn't in the person but in the purpose. The same person can be an arts teacher in one setting and a teaching artist in another. Really great arts teachers include teaching artistry in their practice and pedagogy, and really great teaching artists sometimes serve as teachers of an arts discipline, so the two roles can merge.

Here's a try at illuminating the difference. An art teacher's purpose is to bring learners into an art form to develop basic competence and interest that build increasing skills for a lifelong journey, whether as a professional practitioner or lover of the art form. A teaching artist's purpose is to awaken the artistry of the participants. A teaching artist quickly gets people creating things they care about in an artistic medium, but the goal is not skill development; rather, it's a quality of creative engagement that naturally moves outside the discipline to other parts of life. My first teacher in teaching artistry, the philosopher Maxine Greene, called the teaching artist's goal "wide awakeness." She respected teaching artistry as a way "to awaken persons to a sense of present-ness, to a critical consciousness of what is ordinarily obscured"; she even called it "the capacity to make the familiar strange." She loved that teaching artists lead people "to participate, not simply to contemplate, but to let our energy go out in full encounters…"

A friend heard me going on about this distinction one too many times and challenged me to demonstrate the difference. So, the next day, I taught back-to-back 20-minute classes on the same subject, first as a theater teacher and then as a theater teaching artist. I chose to teach one of the few technical things actors need to study: Shakespearean scansion, which is identifying and respecting the rhythmic patterns of syllabic emphasis in Shakespeare's verse that influence how actors deliver the lines.

ROUND ONE. I was the lively, fun Shakespeare teacher I never had. I introduced the basic rhythmic patterns—iambs, trochees, dactyls, etc.—so we could identify them in modern speech. o-KAY = iamb. DUMB-bell = trochee. We analyzed a sample of Shakespearean text, puzzling over the implications of irregularities. It was interesting to the participants, and all finished knowing more about the subject.

Round two. I began with the question, "Where in life do people naturally use heightened speech?" Some of the answers were "When they're angry" and "When my mother wanted me home for dinner." Next: "What are the ways people heighten their speech? What tools do they naturally use?" I got good answers about word choice, about volume and pitch, about rhythmic changes. I asked for more thinking about those rhythmic patterns: "Can you come up with a line a frustrated mother might say using words that are all in this rhythm: da-DUM?" They came up with: "You GET your BUTT in HERE right NOW." And one that mixes da-DUMs with a DUM-da or two. "Oh MOM, I SWEAR I'll NEV-er EV-er DO that a-GAIN." We tried out other rhythms and discussed what effect they had. Only in the last four minutes did I introduce a bit of Shakespeare's text, encouraging them to see how it had the rhythmic patterns we had been playing with, as well as others.

After I was done, my friend led some reflection with the participants. They said they enjoyed both rounds and felt they got more useful information in the first class. However, they were happy when the first class ended; they felt they'd learned enough. In contrast, they didn't want the second class to end; they felt they had just gotten started and wanted to keep going. During the reflection, they kept noticing and joking about the rhythmic patterns in their speech as they made comments, playfully applying what they'd just learned. At lunch that day, they were still joking about the scansion in one another's speech—and the next day, too.

This demonstrates something that education research tells us about learning (and not just in education settings; the research is deep in business and science as well): it's about *intrinsic* versus *extrinsic* motivation. Intrinsic motivation means engaging for your own personal reasons, driven by your own curiosity or passion to pursue the process' inherent pleasures. Extrinsic motivation means engaging for other people's reasons, pressing along to get an external reward or to avoid punishment, to please someone, or just because everyone else is doing it.

As you know well, in our school lives and our work lives, we are driven mostly by extrinsic motivators. But here's the headline from decades of research: if you are driven by intrinsic motivation in a subject or project, you will always learn more in the long run. That truth shaped my teaching artist choices in the second scansion lesson. The teaching artist guideline is "slow down to speed up": take time to engage personal relevance and curiosity (which are inextricably tied to intrinsic motivation) about a subject, and the learning will go further and deeper in the long run. That's why I began an urban planning workshop about redesigning a neighborhood in San Jose with a map and the question "How would you like creative energy to flow through this area?" instead of "Our budget allows us to renovate one or two buildings as arts centers." It's why starting an eighth-grade history lesson on the music of the Underground Railroad with the question "Where in life do people use music to stay alive?"[21] has more learning impact than starting with "Open

> The teaching artist guideline is "slow down to speed up."

to Chapter Seven." Slow down to speed up—instead of starting with a PowerPoint, open a business meeting by asking everyone to spend three minutes preparing to share what's most important for that meeting, and then watch as a shorter, more effective meeting unfolds. I have worked with organizations that reached out to me because they felt they were being meeting-ed to death, and my teaching artist tools helped make for fewer, faster and more enjoyable meetings. Teaching artistry can also preserve sanity!

There are, in addition to "slow down to speed up," four other teaching artist guidelines at work in that example of my approach to Shakespearean scansion: "a high priority on personal relevance," "tapping innate competence," "scaffolding" and "engagement before information." We'll explore those and a number of other tools in Part Two of this book.

I HAVE SEEN A LOT OF SUPERB teaching artists at work, but the greatest tour de force I've ever witnessed happened in the unlikely setting of a rundown institutional classroom in Indianapolis, Indiana in the late 1980s. The teaching artist was a musician, and there were seven teenage students in his 50-minute workshop. This was his first time working with them and their first time working with each other in this way. That is a tough setup for any teaching artist. This was a special group class, and his goal was to get them to play music together. Each student was both deaf and blind.

As the students were brought in, some in wheelchairs, my mind reeled to find ways he would be able to activate their artistry, the teaching artist's goal, and found none. The teaching artist was relaxed and greeted each student with touch. He gave each a drum and began with one at a time. Striking the drum led each to sense the reverberation on some part of their body. After a time, all seven had the feeling that they could "hear" their own and one another's drum strikes impact on some part of their body. The noise was a thumping cacophony.

He then guided them, by touch, to play in pairs, in rhythmic unison. The students were clearly delighted and experiencing something they had never known before, partnering in sonic rhythm and then varying those rhythms. He built up from pairs to a whole group unison. He had some time left, and he wasn't done. He taught them to play in patterns—one playing four steady beats and the neighbor playing two in the same phrase. They got it. As they worked in pairs, I could see their delight as they came together on the fourth beat.

And then, somehow—and I didn't see how this happened—they began to play as a whole group. Not just following suggested patterns but improvising together. They held the four-beat structure and made musical choices in relation to one another. The sense in the room was ecstasy. They were connecting with one another in a way that they had never experienced in their lives—playfully, creatively, intimately, successfully. Within fifty minutes.

Then the class was over. He said goodbye to each one with a professional musician's acknowledgement offered through touch. He popped his silly little brim-up hat on his head and walked out with me, pleased and relaxed, as cool as musicians can often be. He betrayed no sense that something extraordinary had just happened. The ultimate teaching artist felt only that he just had a good jam session with a group of musicians.

Some Examples of Teaching Artistry in Action

IF YOU GLANCED INTO a teaching artist-led workshop, it wouldn't look weird or different. People sitting in a circle doing something, or small groups bent over an absorbing task. But if you stuck around for a while, you'd start noticing distinctive features. If you stuck around for a culminating event, you'd get the point. Here are four examples.

CARNEGIE HALL launched its pilot of The Lullaby Project[22] in 2011. Their partners at the Jacobi Medical Center wondered if music could help with a challenge their Natal Care Clinic was up against. Many of the women in their care were living in stressful circumstances that inhibited healthy bonding between the mother (or parents) and the newborn, with poorer health outcomes for both. Teaching artists Thomas Cabaniss and Emily Eagen designed a process of guiding each mother to compose (and record) an original lullaby for their child, in just a few hours of enjoyable interaction. The health outcomes of this process have been so positive that there are now spinoff Lullaby Projects in fifty cities across eleven countries. It doesn't matter whether the lullaby is "good" or not; the impact doesn't result from the quality of the noun. The impact comes from the verbs—the activation of artistry and the joy of completing a personally relevant project, as personally relevant as it gets. There is a bounce into stronger family bonding, caregiver well-being and early child development, and the research on Lullaby affirms it. Emotionally, the moms shift from stress to love, from "I can't do this" to surprising successes. (Give yourself a treat: look up the program on the Internet and listen to some of the songs that have been recorded.[23])

WATERBURY, VERMONT is a small rural town, struggling with challenges like every other. Morale grows darker in the long, cold winter months. Teaching artist Gowri Savoor collaborated with a local school art teacher to build a small school residency around a community lantern parade. Interest grew into workshops at the school and community center, where residents young and old designed, built and illuminated lanterns that would be carried on tall sticks through the town on a dark winter night. For weeks, students and adults got together to create their lanterns—including some big ones that took several people to carry—and organize the parade. On a midwinter night, the whole town showed up, complete with bands and onlookers, to march through the town under the lights of their lanterns—A River of Light in Waterbury.[24] The town adopted it as an annual event (as have other towns under Gowri's guidance[25]) supported by the town budget, local businesses and donations from residents, with a different theme each year. They now have a community tradition of hope and connectedness at the hardest time of year.

PUBLIC HIGH SCHOOL STUDENTS in New York City who work with Epic Theatre Ensemble's Remix[26] program study a classic play, like *Hamlet* or *Antigone*. The teaching artists guide the students to explore the play's themes through improvisation and written scenes of their own. They create and perform a "remix" that features original text mixed with student-written scenes that carry their understanding of the relevance of the play to their lives, with a special focus on social justice and equity issues. The performance is supercharged with skillful acting, passionate commitment to the relevant issues and a nuanced understanding of the masterwork. Does this theater-play have an impact? In communities with a 64% high school graduate rate, all—100%—of the students who go through Remix for several years graduate from high school and 97% go on to higher education. All bring a foundation of confidence into their new challenges. And those Epic teaching artists? They keep their professional lives vibrant by mounting productions of plays they are passionate about.

BELGRADE, SERBIA has cut down so many urban trees that it ranks among the lowest tree-cover cities in the world, with serious environmental and quality-of-life consequences. Teaching artists of the Dah Theater devised the Dancing Trees[27] project to draw public attention to the issue as part of their larger "Create Your Own Action" webinar series to encourage civic initiatives. Dancing Trees included free performances of a new immersive dance-theater piece in a park with remaining trees. These led to public roundtable discussions of the issue with climate and urban design experts, activists and artists, to tree-planting events, to a website where the commitment to re-tree Belgrade and other civic initiatives continue and grow.

All four, like all teaching artist work, succeed because teaching artists tap the power of creative engagement to change what's possible, to imagine the world as if it could be otherwise. Maxine Greene notes, "New connections are made in experience: new patterns are formed, new vistas are opened. People see differently, resonate differently."

*

ON MY VERY FIRST DAY as a teaching artist, aged 29, I witnessed the power of those verbs of art that get released by teaching artistry. I was performing in a play on Broadway at the time but had stumbled upon teaching artistry at Lincoln Center, where I explored it during the day. After some training, I took an assignment with a South Bronx fourth-grade classroom. I had done my planning with the classroom teacher I was partnering with, making sure to arrive early on my first day, before classes began. Walking down the second-floor corridor to the classroom, I was more nervous than when walking onto a Broadway stage. There were odd bits of rubble on the hallway floor; I looked up to see paint and plaster peeling from the ceiling. The teacher told me that we would have to start late because someone had broken into the school overnight and smeared human excrement on the walls of her classroom. She and I cleaned the walls with buckets and sponges as the students sat silently and watched. They looked so sad and depleted of energy. I began my lesson feeling that this was the most degraded learning environment for "art" I could imagine.

My lesson was awful—I had more good intent than basic skill. My goal for this first of six visits with them was to have each child select their own superhero aspect, create a superhero mask with a paper plate and crayons and develop and present a stance, a gesture and a voice. They seemed to enjoy the creative steps, making those rudimentary masks that suggested some aspects of their "super" selves with broken crayons on the flimsy white paper plates I'd brought with me. When it was time for each student to present their character—mask, stance, gesture and voice—the smallest kid volunteered to kick things off. I had noticed several of the larger kids bullying and mocking him throughout the class, so I was surprised to see him jump up to be first. Novice that I was, even I had the safeguarding instinct to hold him back, to keep him from being first, but he didn't stop. He leapt into position, held up his paper plate with red markings, pointed to the sky boldly and shouted, "The Avenger." The biggest bully in the class physically recoiled at the power of it; he took a step back and said a quiet "Woah."

There it was, the power of art. The kid who had been pushed around was able to spark an image of power in the bully's mind so vividly that it provoked a visible autonomic response. As raw and undeveloped an artmaking event as it was—in this case, a paper plate, a simplistic creative activity, a kid's theatrical impulses and strong intent—it had enough genuine impact to jangle the status quo. I recall thinking, in that moment, "There is more raw power here than in my NYC actor's life of soap operas, commercials and performing the same play eight times a week on Broadway." I wanted a life radiant with the verbs of art. I had gotten my first taste of activating those verbs in others and witnessing what they can do; I wanted more. And I got decades of it.

The Fundamentals of Teaching Artistry

ARTISTS WHO WORK in communities and schools can enthusiastically name thirty different essential elements of their craft. But they can't boil those down to just a core handful. Even if one teaching artist could, the next one would have a different handful. That's not a solid basis upon which to build a field. So, in 2013, I proposed six essentials of teaching artistry for the U.S. and global field. I stress-tested these six over the subsequent decade to see if they hold true. We used them in the Teaching Artist Development Labs at Lincoln Center (2015-2019) and shared them widely—and they seem to hold water. So, on the basis of wide agreement, here are the six inclinations, understandings, capacities and habits of action that form the Fundamentals of Teaching Artistry.

Activating artistry.

We have already met this one. A teaching artist's number one job is to activate the artistry of others. Once activated, this human power generator (in individuals and groups) can be guided toward accomplishing a wide range of goals.

Adeptness with creative processes.

There is a destination, but it's all about the journey. We launch, guide and open up the treasure and pleasure chest of creative processes. Sure, we care about final products, as all creators do— they add drive and focus to the process and connect it to a wider community and audience. But the teaching artist's specialty is the discovery of the riches along the way, developing a taste for the pleasures found in processes.

Creating safe and brave environments for engagement.

We create environments that are irresistible to join. They are distinctive, even paradoxical (safe but charged)—inviting, challenging, fun, energizing, brave, joyful and sensitively attuned to the participants' cultural backgrounds. We can create those settings quickly and with almost any group of participants. Think about that last sentence for a moment—that's an amazing skill.

Deftness with inquiry.

We don't manage production; we guide exploration. Creative engagement is a co-learning inquiry process, with the teaching artist serving as facilitator, guide and colleague. We help people discover well, setting aside preconceptions and prejudices, to keep the learning process rich with reflection, imagination and wonder, self-assessment, flexible questions, multiple perspectives, mistakes and revision. We begin in interest and curiosity and lead toward making those lifelong habits of mind.

Authenticity.

We live by *The Law of 80%*—eighty percent of what you teach is who you are. Our greatest impact comes from being our artist-selves in the room with participants, openly seeing, responding, discovering and creating connections with what is happening in real time during a project. This is where participants learn the most about what artistry looks and feels like in action. We commit to embodying our curious, positive artist-self in all our choices and actions, and to hold an artist-to-artist co-discovery relationship with participants. This is a serious commitment, sometimes an exhausting one, but it always enriches our own lives as much as it does theirs.

> *Eighty percent of what you teach is who you are.*

Imagining meaningful new worlds.

We yearn toward "the more." We have ready access to the experience of wonder, which transcends understanding, and we can open that in others. We have a relentless urge to reach beyond the literal, beyond "good enough," beyond right answers, standard solutions and existing opinions and judgments to see the world as if it could be otherwise. We live to bring that new world into being.

Why Doesn't Everyone Everywhere Know about Teaching Artistry?

Teaching artistry sounds pretty great, doesn't it? But the professional field has its problems.

It's largely invisible. Even within the arts, lots of people don't know there is such a vocation. There are few good pathways into the field and few reliable ways to build a career that recognizes and rewards increasing skill. The quality of teaching artists' work tends to be high, but quality control is disorganized, and not every teaching artist has basic skills or can deliver as well as those I describe in these pages.

Not least—it's tough to make a living in teaching artistry. You already know that this celebrity-focused world isn't organized to support steady careers for the vast majority of artists. Well, it is even less well-designed to support teaching artists and their commitment to marginalized individuals and communities.

A main reason you don't know about teaching artistry is that it's barely funded at all. This has been the largest frustration of my professional life. Funders are certainly interested in what teaching artists can do, and they support many programs in which teaching artists reliably deliver the goods, year after year after decade, but they don't invest in building the workforce so that it can grow and do more.

In the U.S., Grantmakers in the Arts (GIA) is a beloved service organization for funders who care about the arts. After years of suggestion and lobbying, I nudged GIA into creating a one-day summit to address the issue of funding the field of teaching artistry in the U.S. About fifteen of the largest funders flew to St. Louis to meet with some senior teaching artists and program directors. We gave it our best advocacy effort, hyperaware that this was a once-in-a-lifetime opportunity. After the warmups and introductory presentations, real discussions began. Funders acknowledged that they completely rely on the teaching artist workforce to fulfill the goals of many of the programs they fund—for some funders, teaching artists are central to *all* of their funded programs. They acknowledged that they spend next to nothing to build, advance or sustain the workforce they rely on. These open admissions were promising. But when challenged to state why they offered no support, they waffled. Their explanations sounded lame even to them: "It is a hybrid job and doesn't fit conveniently into our funding categories." "We think of teaching artists as school-based, and we don't fund schools, just communities and social outcomes." (Me: "But you know they aren't just school-based." Them: "I know, but that's how our foundation thinks.") "Our Board doesn't want to fund artists, even though we rely on them for all our innovative work." They looked embarrassed. At the end of that day, we challenged them to identify ways to change a status quo that they recognized was mistaken, counterproductive and basically stupid. They offered a few tepid suggestions, and then admitted they weren't going to follow through on taking even those weak actions. The day and event ended with exactly no impact or advancement. What prosaic, bureaucratic reasons to starve such a force for positive change.

Imagining What's Possible

I F WE AS A SOCIETY could adequately support our teaching artists, here are some flashes of what could become possible. My imagining here is mostly based in my home country, but these ideas could make a difference anywhere in the world.

Social prescribing, whereby doctors can prescribe arts activities for health outcomes. This already exists in the U.K., and there are some pilot projects sprouting in the U.S. Because it works. For many medical conditions, physical and psychological, engaging in the arts is at least as effective as taking prescription drugs, with no negative side effects and at lower cost. For mild depression caused by loneliness or loss, a doctor might prescribe that you take a group clay sculpture workshop. For your arthritis, she can prescribe an aquatics dance class. Every natal clinic in the U.S. could have a Lullaby Project. If insurance covered such prescriptions in the U.S., teaching artists would offer cleverly designed workshops to address a wide range of medical needs. The country would be healthier and happier, and individuals, governments and insurance companies would save billions of dollars that are currently spent on less effective pharmacological remedies.

Creativity coaches. Public school systems are in multiple crises: achievement gaps, low student motivation, high drop-out rates, behavioral challenges—not to mention teacher discouragement and burnout. Every educator knows that engaged students learn more, learn better, collaborate better and come to love learning. (Or rather, come *back* to loving learning in a school setting; every young person loves learning about the things that interest them.) Yet the schooling industries and school boards continue to insist on outworn teaching methods and relentlessly boring school days. If school boards prioritized student engagement, as they do in Finland, the world's number one academically achieving nation, we would see many of our educational and social problems lessen. Every school could have a teaching artist as a creativity coach to help each faculty member rethink the way they teach the material in their curriculum. In fact, Vermont has been experimenting with this idea for the past decade in its Community Engagement Lab,[28] where teaching artists are poised to deliver this work and to set a national example. For our students, our teachers, our schools and our communities, the benefits would be incalculable.

Teaching artist response teams inside disaster situations and displaced-person and refugee camps. Every major disaster response operation should place teaching artists at the planning table and in the field with those affected. Every major refugee center needs teaching artists at work with residents, even if the individuals and families are there for only short-term stays. You already know why. Recovery is not just about survival essentials, buildings and material possessions. People whose lives have been upended, many of whom have been through terrifying experiences, need the healing experiences that personal artistic engagement provides. The "flow experience" of creative engagement is inherently healing. After the initial period of dealing with basic safety and survival needs, displaced people need regular creative expression and satisfaction to restore wellbeing, to find connection and to experience rehumanization; they need the engagement with beauty that teaching artists bring. A few refugee centers do provide workshops with teaching artists, and staff members in those settings will tell you how much difference it makes. Read about the Dream Orchestra in Sweden (mentioned earlier) where unaccompanied minors who got to Sweden through horrific journeys find their new family in the orchestra they join. Celebrate the profound work of Musicians without Borders in locations of war, armed conflict and displacement.[29] Study *Art Became the Oxygen*,[30] a report from the U.S. Department of Arts and Culture[31] (not a government agency but a community artist collective—"If the federal government won't create a cabinet position, let's create our own") which shares more on the subject.

Offices of artistic engagement at the United Nations, the World Bank, the International Monetary Fund, the International Rescue Committee, the World Health Organization, the Children's Defense Fund, the Red Cross and Red Crescent, and more. I can picture the nameplate on an open door: Director of Creative Engagement. Only with the regular *inside* presence of teaching artists can the power of universal personal artistry find its way into improving projects in a thousand small and not-so-small ways.

Teaching artistry as a required course in all teacher education programs. What a difference it would make if every new teacher learned about the pleasures and powers of creative engagement while learning how to "control" a classroom. Most troublesome behaviors in classrooms disappear if students are regularly involved in creatively interesting projects—you know this truth simply from knowing

Most troublesome behaviors in classrooms disappear if students are regularly involved in creatively interesting projects.

young people and having been a young person. I'm not suggesting that state-mandated curricula be changed (good luck with that, in any case). I'm simply suggesting that, as teachers-in-training learn how to deliver the curriculum they will be required to teach, whatever it is, they also learn how to activate students' personal enthusiasm.

A teaching artist component in the professional training pathways of medicine, policing and criminal justice, MBAs, public policy, political science and law—not to teach the arts, but to vitalize creativity in the profession, to humanize communication and to emphasize ambiguity tolerance and reflective practice. Even in the arts—how deeply I wish conductors, stage directors, visual artists, choreographers and arts administrators, to name a few, would blend teaching artistry into their learning pathways. The arts would bring a very different value to the wider public if they had teaching artist habits of mind available alongside their arts-discipline-trained habits of mind. How often I have heard the complaint, "It's so frustrating; what's wrong with them? The public should love opera; baroque music; Merce Cunningham dances; etc." No, there's no should about it. Engage people in what is truly relevant and valuable, and maybe they will buy tickets. You need teaching-artist thinking to change the relationship to the public. It's proven—it's just not prioritized.

Festivals of the participatory arts. In addition to festivals that celebrate what great artists can do, let's have whole festivals that celebrate what all of us can do when guided well. (Burning Man is an extreme embodiment of this impulse.) Only a few can play as well as the jazz greats during a festival, and we delight in what they can do. But all of us can have one hell of a great time messing around inside jazz when well-guided by a teaching artist; and I can guarantee that those of us who do so will be more jazzed to appreciate what the greats can do. See my example on page 81 of what that can look like.

A new federal WPA in the U.S. In the New Deal of the 1930s, the Works Project Administration hired artists to work on community projects, in all the arts, to lift a disheartened public out of its literal and metaphoric depression. Their impact was disproportionately powerful and positive. Imagine today's teaching artists working with communities on local environmental and health challenges; bringing rural towns together in celebrations; deployed in high-crime communities and in juvenile justice settings to reduce crime and prison sentences; honoring and building recognition for the work of overlooked public servants ... dream with me. A number of colleagues, notably writer/activist Arlene Goldbard, have written about this idea, and national Democratic Party circles have floated some actual policy proposals in the last decade. We can see the beginnings of this idea in ArtistYear,[32] a national service program for newly graduated teaching artists to expand arts learning in schools that need it.

Peacebuilding. Artist exchanges are sometimes used by governments to thaw international hostilities or to build goodwill through tours. What about teaching artist-led projects that bring individuals from opposing groups together—for example, Combatants for Peace,[33] made of Palestinian and Israeli theater artists? What about teaching artist exchanges, where they engage with community members who can "make stuff they care about" across cultures? Imagine a teaching artist in a closed country like North Korea or Myanmar, using their skills to make something universally human with its citizens. The international community could create a Creativity Corps (like the Peace Corps), perhaps run out of the United Nations.

What We Could Do with a Big Investment

HERE ARE FIVE THINGS we could do to build this field if a visionary funder plonked down a significant investment.

1. Collect good data. There has been only one national study of teaching artistry in the U.S. (in 2011);[34] there is also some data from the ArtWorks Alliance[35] in the U.K. and a bit of additional information about the field scattered about. With support, this field could strengthen its foundations by getting better information about itself. We don't know, even roughly, how many professional teaching artists there are. In the U.S., some say 10,000 and others say 30,000; around the world, some say 30,000 and others say 100,000. We could gather an inventory of training opportunities, major programs and existing research. We could use seed money for academic research on impact. A substantive effort to collect basic data would professionalize the field. An inventory and searchable archive of successful projects would help make it vividly real and relevant.

2. Create early pathways in. There are few reliable pathways into the field, and too few young artists hear about teaching artistry before they graduate. They enter the real world and realize how narrow their preparation has been. I have heard their outrage many times: "Why didn't they teach me about this before I graduated? Now it's so much harder to begin."

I DREAM OF MAKING compelling introductory materials about teaching artistry and getting them in front of every young and emerging artist. We could make partnership agreements with organizations that develop young artists, committing them to include a substantive introduction to teaching artistry in every young artist's beginnings, right in the orientation week. The materials would plant the seed that an artist's career can grow wider and create more impact (and more income) in the world through teaching artistry. Show them the possibilities right at the "stem cell" stage of their careers. Partnerships are not just for supply, but also for demand. Partnerships are the only way to invigorate demand from sectors outside the arts, as advocacy and visibility reveal the proven benefits. We need strong introductory materials for non-arts organizations, strong stories that let them know what opportunities they are missing, what teaching artists are and can do, and what they could accomplish by working with teaching artists.

3. Support continual improvement. A well-designed course series—online, in-person or both—could help active teaching artists hone and improve their practice. Online learning may not be optimum, but it has advantages. Here's a possible series of ten courses. Why think small?

    i. BEGINNING WELL.

    ii. DEEPENING YOUR PRACTICE.

    iii. TEACHING ARTISTRY IN EDUCATION SETTINGS.

    iv. WORKING WITH SPECIAL OPPORTUNITIES
    (for example, people with disabilities or older people/ creative aging).

    v. TEACHING ARTISTRY FOR SOCIAL IMPACT.
    (This one actually exists, created by ITAC.[36] We know there is interest in online learning: over 296 registered for this course in its first six weeks.)

    vi. THE ENTREPRENEURIAL TEACHING ARTIST
    (including how to fundraise).

vii. Working in Health and Wellness.

viii. Working for Social Justice and Democracy.

ix. Becoming an Effective Ambassador for Teaching Artistry.

x. Leadership: Developing the field in large and small ways.

4. Create live model projects that people can visit, to show what's possible. Seeing and feeling a good example is uniquely potent in advocacy. This was certainly true for the worldwide embrace of music for social change projects. So many grew from direct contact with the El Sistema[37] program in Venezuela and its world-touring top orchestras, which gave electrifying demonstrations of what's possible in concert halls around the world. El Sistema Venezuela has an extensive video and written archive, but the work isn't infectious and inspiring in documented form, and the archive is too big to explore easily. José Antonio Abreu, the founder of El Sistema, had a firm practice with potential supporters: "Come and see the work first. Then we'll talk." This practice converted me. I had been a skeptic before my first visit to Venezuela, but in the first hour of direct contact, I realized I was witnessing one of the most extraordinary achievements in the history of the arts. So, when I talked with Abreu, we had a very different conversation.

How incredibly useful it would be to have clear, visible examples that answer questions like: What does great teaching artistry look like? What does it look like in the development of artists? What does great work in creative aging look like? In refugee communities? In hospitals and in prisons?

5. Launch a development team. A team of professionals hired to do three things: 1) Gather and distribute information about existing funding opportunities that invite, or might include, teaching artist proposals; 2) Advocate and imagine with funders—few funders ever think about teaching artistry, and we could find ways to get them to explore ways teaching artists can help them and explicitly include teaching artists in their grant descriptions; and 3) Develop partnerships with mission-driven organizations that discover that teaching artists can help them achieve their goals in uniquely powerful ways.

An example of how closed the door has been, and how significant one little crack can be: my wife, Tricia Tunstall, was invited to the World Bank Headquarters in Washington, D.C. to do presentations about teaching artistry's potential contributions to the United Nations' Sustainable Development Goals. Her participants were excited at the power of the possibilities. At the end of the half-day, one of the top executives said to her, "I have spent twenty-five years working on major projects that address the life-and-death needs of millions of people, and today is the first time I have ever even had the thought that the arts might have something to contribute."

We have a long way to go. Teaching artistry has so much to contribute, but it can't do so from behind a closed door.

Part Two:
Teaching Artist Tools and Guidelines

PART TWO OF THIS BOOK DIGS into the *how* of teaching artistry, its tools and its goals. Educators may think that these guidelines are strikingly similar to guidelines for great teaching in general. It's true. Take great teaching skills, blend in the skills and knowledge of an artist, and you get teaching artistry. George Bernard Shaw famously insulted teachers with his quip, "Those who can, do. Those who can't, teach." As I see it, those who can, do. Those who can do two things are teaching artists.

Before we dig in, a bit of context by way of a story. Years ago, I slammed into a bad professional moment while being interviewed on live television by a peppy morning talk show host. Near the end of the interview, she said, "Eric, we have just a couple of minutes left, so can you wrap this up for us with a quick, clear distinction between art and entertainment?"

I had no idea how to respond. In a panic, I did what people sometimes do, which is grab a random strategy and stick with it, even if it doesn't make much sense. The strategic lifejacket I clung to was a hazy recollection of once being told, "If you are ever dying on live television, just don't stop talking, so they can't turn it into sound bites that will haunt you for the rest of your life." That's all I had. So, two interminable minutes of meaningless blather poured out of me—but there were no pauses.

Immediately afterward, I set out to answer that question for myself so that I would never be stuck like that again. What *is* the distinction between art and entertainment? Why is entertainment so omnipresent and art seemingly so rarified and elite? The answer I arrived at has served well. The distinction doesn't lie in "the thing" you are looking at. Art and entertainment aren't opposites, just as good conversations and great conversations aren't opposites.

Entertainment is distinguished by our experience of it, which happens within what we already know. Whatever our reaction (laughing, crying, getting excited or scared), the experience confirms our sense of the way the world is or should be. It feels great to have skilled people go to great lengths to fashion entertainments that confirm our personal way of seeing things. We pay big money for that.

Art, on the other hand, happens outside of what we already know. Inherent in the artistic experience is the capacity to create a new sense of how the world is or might be. That experience of expanding our sense of what's possible *is* the artistic experience. Art is a verb. Creating a new sense of how the world is or might be takes imagination; it's a creative act. It takes artistry to do it—the artistry that all of us brim with, the artistry that teaching artists specialize in activating.

You may notice that my definition of the arts experience—expanding to create personally relevant connections beyond what you already know—is pretty much identical to a definition of learning, or making new connections outside of what you already know. So, the term *teaching artist* makes sense, right? Actually, it's redundant.

The Tools of Teaching Artistry

HERE ARE SOME TOOLS used by teaching artists around the world. This includes artists who have never heard the term "teaching artist" but have a history of working with local communities and schools. Teaching artists don't use every tool on every occasion, but they keep them at the ready to use with the widest range of participants, for the wide range of purposes that teaching artists address. (We will look into those purposes after introducing the tools.)

Individual teaching artists use these tools in their own style. For any given project, they use a mix of new ideas and their trusted reliables to fit the particular opportunity. Each time, the mix of activities has to be just right—for this purpose, with this group, in this setting.

It's important for teaching artists to experiment with new material on every occasion because of the Law of 80%. Remember that? Eighty percent of what you teach is who you are. In trying out new material every time, teaching artists model the risk-taking and curiosity they want their participants to emulate. They aren't cranking out a nifty workshop that always works; they are launching a meaningful inquiry they want to explore with others involved. The teaching artist version of the mantra "Be the change you want to see in the world" is "Be the adventurous learner you want your participants to be."

Let's look at some guidelines of teaching artistry in practice.

Set up and shut up.

THE TEACHING ARTIST sets up a challenge, clearly and cleverly, and then lets the creative action unfold without a lot of instruction. The creative action by the participants holds the learning, not the talking or "teaching" around it. A good activity sparks the impulse to engage, the challenge perfectly targeting the interests and skill level of the particular group. In setting up activities, I don't use the word "art" much anymore; it carries too much baggage about elitism and fancy buildings and can be a debilitating tripwire for those who don't yet recognize their own natural artistry. I tend to say, "Make stuff you care about," because that's what we do in any medium when our artistry is engaged. The teaching artist sets up the challenge and then lets the participants take it and run.

Slow down to speed up.

WE MET THIS GUIDELINE in the Shakespearean scansion activity I described. If we take time for participants to find their own relevant place in the material being introduced, if we engage them experientially first, we activate their curiosity and artistry, which is the gateway to intrinsic motivation. Remember, intrinsic motivation will always lead to greater learning and accomplishment in the long run than compulsion or compliance will.

Engagement before information.

TEACHING ARTISTS DON'T front-load information and explanation; they first engage participants in the subject area with the fun of a creative challenge. When people accept a creative invitation and things go well and they make stuff they care about, when they immerse themselves in those challenges, they become curious to know more. It just happens, reliably. You know it from your own life experience—when you emerge from completing something interesting, even something small, questions and ideas arise and you have the impulse to talk and think about it more. Information gets shared and pursued in answer to those curiosities; those are teachable moments. If information is shared in response to curiosity, it is taken in more deeply and remembered longer. That information isn't meant to "cover" a subject area but rather to deepen relevance, interest and motivation. So, educators of the world, you win at the engagement game *and* at the information game if you engage first. As Arthur Costa, the cofounder of the Institute for Habits of Mind, said, "For the brain to comprehend, the heart must listen first."

High priority on personal relevance.
TEACHING ARTISTS KNOW the work goes faster and further if it is carefully grounded in things that matter to the people involved. We can't tell people what should be relevant to them (although that is almost universally done in education and the arts, without much success). We can't make casual assumptions about individual relevance and get full engagement—every individual has their own private world of significance and value. For engagement, teaching artists invite people's personal stories and experiences, not their opinions, into the beginning of a process. Information activates the head; stories activate the heart. All artists know that strong art springs from experience, from the heart, gut and spirit—so that's how teaching artists draw people into a project. A good teaching artist who's working with a group on the climate crisis doesn't focus on general nature or climate concerns; they focus on the climate issues that are directly impacting that particular group.

Observation before interpretation.
PEOPLE LOVE THEIR OPINIONS. They build their identities around them. They jump to lay them out, to express their preferences, as a first and often only response (an instinct reinforced by social media). But wide-awakeness gets lost in the opine forest. Teaching artists guide people around the dead ends of their preconceptions and judgements, their snap likes and dislikes, into detailed

observation. It's astonishing how hard this is for people to do. We are so conditioned to celebrate instant judgment and strong opinions that we grow uncomfortable in moments of uncertainty. (When I hear absolute pronouncements about complex topics, I always picture smug Roman emperors enjoying their thumbs-up or -down verdicts at the Colosseum.) Teaching artists build ambiguity tolerance: "Let's observe what's here before we start judging it or interpreting it." They seek to build observational skills as habits of mind, to counter the instant "opinion" gratification that Western cultures (and social media) inculcate.

IF THIS INTERESTS YOU, there is a practice you might want to study: Visual Thinking Strategies.[38] VTS was developed over thirty years ago at New York's Museum of Modern Art by Philip Yenawine and developmental psychology researcher Abigail Housen. Its deceptively simple practice deflects snap judgment and ungrounded interpretation by relying on three questions asked of those who are observing artworks: *What's going on in this artwork? What do you see that makes you say that? What more can you find?* This approach dramatically changes the observation and discovery process. VTS has been applied to medical training, where it helps doctors learn how to observe symptoms, as mentioned earlier. Teaching artist researcher Alexa Miller[39] discovered that wrong diagnoses are often the result of doctors' inability to tolerate ambiguity; there is status (and efficiency) in making quick, authoritative judgments, and most doctors aren't comfortable with uncertainty. In a Harvard Medical School study, Miller led sessions wherein med school students looked at paintings and learned to slow down and carefully observe their features. They found that this training transferred to more detailed medical observation, leading to different, richer, wiser interpretations of patient symptoms. Diagnoses get sharper with more care and curiosity in perceiving. Ambiguity tolerance is a life skill that applies in many professional environments; surveys of corporate leaders identify it as a key skill for success in the modern work environment. (The same surveys also rate creativity as a top essential skill.) Without rolling my teaching artist's eyes, let me ask if ambiguity tolerance might be important in our personal lives? You'd better believe it is.

Scaffolding.

TEACHING ARTISTRY borrows this metaphor from construction work, referring to platforms set up at different levels around a building. Scaffolding enables workers to complete projects at one floor level and then step up to work on the next. Teaching artists "scaffold" their creative activities in the same way. They break them into steps, each of which is fun and interesting and provides a sense of completion—with its bounce of increased interest to take the next step.

Here is an example of scaffolding from a lesson intended to increase appreciation of Mozart's music; thanks to the great teaching artist Judy Hill Bose for some of the ideas in this sequence.

To many people not in the "Art Club," Mozart's piano music is mildly attractive, tinkly fluff, something like fussy wallpaper. In this activity, participants watch a live performance of a short Mozart solo piano selection. It doesn't have much impact. Then we start the teaching artist's preparatory activities. Participants take a partner and a first challenge—to walk a set cross-the-room path in the workshop space together, one pair at a time with others watching. Partner A "walks in an interesting way" as Partner B walks alongside them, studying the walk. Then each pair does their paired walk again, but this time Partner B "accompanies" A's walk in an interesting way. The group watches all the paired walks and then creates a list of all the different ways that Bs accompanied their partner—e.g., they followed, they ran ahead, they pushed, they went higher and lower, they mirrored, they blocked, etc. The pairs are then assigned to compose and perform a less-than-60-second piece on the air piano. (Everyone can play the air piano brilliantly, often with great flair.) In the composition, the right hand plays the melody, and the left hand must use at least three of those different kinds of accompaniment we noted from the prior exercise. Each person composes and rehearses with their back to their partner, and then turns and performs for their partner, with the partner noting the different kinds of left-hand accompaniment in feedback after. We then return to a performance of the same Mozart selection we heard 15 minutes earlier. The listening experience is radically different, fascinated, punctuated by laughter at some of Mozart's clever ideas. The fussy wallpaper has become a discovery center. They want more.

Through those scaffolded steps, the participants go from disinterest to fascinated discovery in a few minutes. The walking exercise gently challenges them to invent and present their own solution to an odd but slightly interesting challenge—aimed to push them a little beyond comfort, prompting them to make specific choices with a sense of fun and success. The list of accompanying styles the group gathers is owned by the group—it's *their* list, not some Mozart expert's. The air piano challenge invites their playful creativity and dramatic performance moments; there's a lot of laughter in the room. But they were artistically engaged in real musical thinking throughout, making choices directly related to choices Mozart made, refining their choices as Mozart did, making a comic-but-intentional piece with a beginning-middle-end. Do you see how each scaffolded step was complete and satisfying in itself? How each step set them up for a related but different challenge in the next step, and built enough confidence to dig into a playful compositional challenge they would never have thought possible 15 minutes earlier? The result of this series of steps: a radically altered experience of Mozart. Which is what I was hired to deliver.

The ruthless use of fun.

ALL LIVING THINGS—from amoeba to zebra, with humans somewhere in the mix—turn *toward* that which is pleasurable in some way, and turn *away* from that which is not. Teaching artists use fun, not as a sugar-coating on a good-for-you-but-dull-or-necessary activity, but as the nature of the work itself. The questions good teaching artists ask are inherently interesting, enjoyable to mess around with. The activities are inviting or irresistible. They expand the palette of pleasures that people can access.

A group of civic leaders I worked with in Nashville's leadership development program had never known the pleasures of improvising an argument over who gets to sit in a chair, or in imagining a scene they might write in a play about that chair argument—but after twenty hilarious minutes in my workshop,

> Teaching artists use fun [...] as the nature of the work itself.

they knew something new about themselves as both improvisers and playwrights. Then two teaching artist colleagues performed the meeting scene between Petruchio and Kate in Shakespeare's *The Taming of the Shrew* for the group, and they recognized, in a way they hadn't in high school English class, how outrageous it is. We then applied the learning from these playful activities to the work of a creative economy in Nashville. Notice the scaffolding? The 75-minute workshop engaged them in several kinds of fun and brought out abilities they didn't know they had, right up to and through the imagining of how to increase the creative pleasure and effectiveness of the people they oversee in their offices.

Great questions.

ASKING GREAT QUESTIONS and facilitating exciting discussions are advanced teaching artist skills. When I observe a teaching artist, these are clear indicators of their level of mastery. My project with Her Majesty's Education Inspectorate in Scotland was to develop observable indicators of creative teaching; we identified the nature of the questions being asked and engagement levels during discussions as key clues. We looked for questions with an emotional bite, innately interesting questions, questions we found ourselves answering before we realized it.

Not all teachers of teaching artistry are as absolute with this guideline as I am: a teaching artist must never ask a question that has a single correct answer. People, especially people in schools, are so marinated in single-right-answer thinking in our culture that they are taken over by their conditioning, which is antithetical to the inner state teaching artists must encourage. Artistry celebrates the multiplicity of answers and perspectives, thriving on questions of quality, personal connectedness and experimentation. We need to protect a fragile aesthetic inquiry against the bullying power of right-answering, which people snap into instantly because it is reinforced throughout our lives. Great questions work differently in us. The question "What do you take as evidence of learning?" redirected the trajectory of my whole career. "The earth is speaking, how do we respond?" "Where in life do people use music to stay alive?" "What are you noticing here that you think no one else is seeing?" "What should be the first sentence of your autobiography?"—I led a weeklong workshop that addressed that question.

Remember that fourth Fundamental? "Deftness with inquiry." Teaching artists know how to delve, reframe and provoke discovery of relevance, how to spark assessment by asking questions. Fun questions, interesting, surprising, incisive, deceptively simple questions. Socratic dialogue meets genuine curiosity.

Enabling constraints.

A LIMITATION, IF WE GET IT JUST RIGHT, frees us to go deeper and succeed more fully. Painters know what size canvas is just right for the painting they have envisioned; or they shape their ideas to work on the canvas they happen to have. A composer's commission may require a 15-minute piece.

I first heard the term "enabling constraint" from Thomas Cabaniss, the teaching artist who co-devised The Lullaby Project. In those sessions, teaching artists present a few guiding constraints that enable "non-musical" mothers to compose a lullaby for their new baby in just a couple of hours.

Here is how enabling constraints work. If you ask a six-year-old boy to draw a self-portrait, he will draw a stick figure or generally oval-shaped humanoid, and maybe a house and sun—but that activity doesn't engage his artistry or generate satisfaction because the assignment isn't well-targeted for his skill level. But if you ask him to draw three lines on his page, each of which captures a different feeling he has had today, he puzzles for a moment. Remembering his annoying sister at breakfast, he draws a dark jagged line. Remembering the butterfly outside the school building, he makes a light curvy line. Remembering his math homework, he makes a dense little mess. The constraints of the assignment free him to apply his innate artistry, personally and successfully. He invests his own experience in creative choices about line drawing right at the edge of his developmental capacity. The constraint sets him up to succeed, to engage his artistry, where the open assignment doesn't. Teaching artists are masters at designing enabling constraints within the scaffolded steps of their work.

Tap competence.

TWO TRUTHS COMBINE HERE: 1) All learning is built upon previous learning, and 2) Everyone is artistically capable.

Teaching artists tap that innate capability (in playful and clever ways) and then scaffold small creative success upon creative success. Soon, participants find their way into creative flow, making things they care about.

Most people over age nine believe they are artistically incompetent in most areas (younger children feel they are basically omnicompetent in all the arts: "My drawing of a cow belongs in a museum, or at least on the refrigerator door.") The over-nines may not be able to draw a good cow or belt out an aria, but they're not incompetent. Though they may have blocked or disowned their inherent basic abilities, a good teaching artist can come in under the radar alert of "I don't do this" and engage them in simple activities that tap their innate competence. For example, a teaching artist might—avoiding tripwire words like *choreography*—offer interesting challenges to be solved by natural physical movement; in a few minutes, the participant is making choreographic choices without any dance vocabulary being used. Another example: when I gathered my working group at Tanglewood to design the summer's interactive family concerts, we began by listing all the things we could safely assume almost everyone in the audience could do musically, at any age or skill level—abilities we could bring into fun musical activities. We identified about 50 basic competencies everyone has that we might tap.

Knowing when to use arts vocabulary.

THE FIRST RULE HERE IS: *not at the start*. If you introduce the art term at the beginning, the work becomes "learning about" that term. Starting with "Today we will learn about sonata form" creates distance, implying "I will teach you about an important feature of my art form today that you *should* know about, and I will try to make it interesting." By contrast, teaching artists begin by activating artistry in a hands-on way, guiding participants to use their creative competence in small projects that focus on particular and interesting challenges. In the teaching artist version of the Shakespearean scansion workshop described earlier, I didn't use the word "scansion" until near the end. In the theater teacher version of that experiment, "scansion" appeared in the first sentence.

Balance the focus on process and focus on product.
THE U.S. AND MOST WESTERN countries are overwhelmingly product- and results-minded—not just a little, but insanely so. (Unhealthily so, in my view.) We "go for the gold," want to "get to the finish," put all our energy on the product. Teaching artists recognize that final products are important (all artists want to complete their works!), but they know that all the learning gold, all the transformative experience, opens up in the creative process. Teaching artists guide a group's attention so that processes get recognized, explored and enjoyed as much as products do.

Reflection.
THE PHILOSOPHER JOHN DEWEY nailed it: "If we do not reflect on our experiences, we do not learn from them." Reflective skills and habits of mind are the most stinted essentials in conventional arts learning. Western cultures are belligerently anti-reflective, conditioning us to speed to the payoff and get the gratification, period. Yet all the potential for learning and for change lies in the uncertain (liminal) zones, and we must reflect on those elusive experiences to harvest what they hold.

Good teaching artists bring as much creative flair to reflection as they do to their activities. They have to, as it is basically remedial work. Reflection is full of subtle pleasures—like discovering something you are good at, or catching how you did something you hadn't noticed before, or appreciating the quality of choices you made without thinking. Teaching artists guide participants toward those subtle new delights. We want you to come back to those pleasures again and again. I wrote an essay on the natural joys of reflection three decades ago; it's at least as relevant now than it was then.[40]

Self-assessment.

IN ALL LEARNING, *self*-assessment is the most important kind. Other forms of feedback—testing, objective scoring, a teacher's objective analysis, even a beloved mentor's observations—can be powerful, but they contribute best, in the long run, when added to accurate and growth-oriented self-assessment.

That's not how schools or most institutions work, of course. They believe that independent tests or the judgments of someone in charge are the assessments that matter, even though convenience and control tend to drive evaluation practices more than belief in their efficacy. Real success in the long journey of improvement requires that we get good at knowing the quality of our own work and then developing a sense of direction toward "better." We make hundreds of decisions in every creative process, often tiny ones. They are guided by our individual sense of better and worse, by our assessment of each choice and its consequences. (Consider: you make thirty such adjustments a minute when driving a car, and that's not even creative—at least, I hope it isn't.)

Teaching artists hold their opinions back to prioritize participants' reliance on their own assessments, both along the way and at the end. In fact, I instruct teaching artists to curb even their instinctive praises of "good job," "I love that," and "awesome"—because, well-intentioned as those accolades may be, they don't really help participants. Good teaching artists carefully build the skills and habits of accurate self-assessment, instilling confidence in those observations to deepen creative strength over time. In working with professional actors, teachers and teaching artists over decades, I am always humbled at how little I can actually teach them. Most of their professional improvement comes from their own small choices and not my instruction. The best I can do is affirm clarity and aspiration toward the right goals, a taste for accurate assessment and habits of growth-mindset, and then support them toward continual improvement.

Prioritize moments of personal choice.

PICASSO FAMOUSLY DECLARED that every act of creation is first an act of destruction. In making a choice, we kill off the other choices we might have made. Sometimes bold artists dare to behead settled certainties in their art forms—Duchamp submitted his famous urinal as "Fountain" to an art show in 1917. Even harder, we sometimes must choose to delete a brilliant, beloved idea of our own because it doesn't fit exactly right. That can feel bad; artists sometimes speak of having to "kill their babies." But choice is a powerful act.

[T]here is power in the moment of conscious choice.

Even if a particular choice doesn't work out in the long run, there is power in the moment of conscious choice. You've experienced the sequence: looking up toward the ceiling or sky while considering a choice, and then... the moment of choice. And down comes your gaze into action. Teaching artists set people up to notice and benefit from that power, to acknowledge and celebrate the act of choice-making, so that the participant feels the resonance of the moment.

Presenting creative work makes us vulnerable; many people are nervous to present, fearing negative response. Teaching artists know how to manage this sensitivity. In carefully guiding a group to give feedback, I start by outlawing comments about liking and disliking, and in place of that, I propose, "Let's name some of the choices we noticed she made in the work." I watch for and blunt their comments of preference and judgment, focusing them simply on, "What choices did she make?" Participants offer a parade of answers. This recognition matters to the person who shared their work. Then, after affirming many of those acts of choice, I add, "What were the consequences of some of those choices we noticed?"

Choice and consequence. You could spend a lifetime applying that pair of bifocal reflective lenses—a responsible, honest, engaged lifetime. In my experience, as we get practiced in attending to the mini-theater of choice, people get better at making good choices in the larger theater of life.

With advanced participants, I add the concept of *lineage* for further reflection: *Where did that choice come from in you; what is its lineage? What in your cultural and personal background led to that choice?* That takes the inquiry deeper. The awareness of cultural influences brightens. Attending to one's choice-consequence lineage is a habit of mind that eases the grip of prejudice and social conditioning.

Routines and Rituals that Support Teaching Artist Practice

MANY TEACHING ARTISTS develop routines and rituals for their participants, especially for groups they see over time. What gets repeated gets remembered. These tools can make an impression even in short-term relationships.

What's the difference between a ritual and a routine? There is a lot of overlap, but rituals generally intend to change inner states while routines focus on outer states. Routines increase efficiency and can develop a kind of elegance in getting necessary things done. A group that takes ownership of a set-up or clean-up routine builds group identity through the shared responsibility. (Quick etymology break—etymologically, *to respond* means *to promise back*. So, *responsibility* means *the capacity to promise, to give a personal commitment, back to others*.) Over time, a routine requires less conscious energy, allowing the teaching artist to add subtle aesthetic qualities, like "Let's try it in silence today" or "Try saying one word to each person you make eye contact with as you set up today."

Rituals lead into (and sometimes out of) the spirit of the environment the group creates together. A ritual affirms the inner space of meeting; it embodies the shared values and worldview of the group. Developing a ritual with a group is a powerful tool; the feel of a group's atmosphere is often remembered long after the actual activities are forgotten. Here are a few examples.

BRAVO POLICY. When the word "bravo" was first used in English-speaking theaters, it was not called out in recognition of dazzling virtuosity as it is now. It was called out in recognition of great courage. When someone performed an act of courage under the pressure of the public gaze, spectators cried out "Bravo!" whether the execution was perfect or not. Some teaching artists ask their participants to say "bravo" when they see someone take a courageous action in the work. Everyone pauses briefly while the speaker describes the bravery they are recognizing in the other person's action, and then everyone goes back to work. Not a big deal, but the regular honoring of courage counterbalances the usual overemphasis on accomplishment. This ritual empowers and celebrates those who aren't as skilled as the impressive few who usually get all the attention. The act of acknowledgement is impactful. I know that personally: when someone calls "bravo" for a move I've made as their workshop leader, even for the experienced elder that I am, it's always touching.

BEST MISTAKE OF THE DAY. In this ritual, at the end of every workshop or class, the teaching artist leaves a few minutes for participants to nominate their blunders and fumbles of the day for consideration. The group votes on the best—i.e., the one that produced the most learning—and they give it a cheer. This increases the boldness of risk-taking in the workshop over time, as mistakes lose their sting, getting taken in playful stride.

WARM-UP ACTIVITIES. These provide quick, playful, experiential introductions to the main work that follows. Though every teaching artist has their favorite warm-ups, which they adapt to the particulars of each setting, they invent new ones too. They are often game-like. For example, slow-motion tag, which could be a good exercise for a dance or theater workshop in staying real within an artificial performance style. Slow-motion tag challenges you to keep the game's motivations—to tag or to avoid being tagged—fully active, even as you add the playful constraint of never breaking super-slow movement, right down to facial expressions. It's fun, it's inclusive because it suspends the usual hierarchy of physical ability, *and* it sets up an exploration of deep artistic questions about genuineness within artificial conventions. The group might then explore how to act truthfully in Shakespearean language or in the language of ballet. Another example from colleagues at AIM (Academy for Impact through Music) where these ideas are finding new forms: a group stands in a circle, and the teaching artist, without a word, establishes a four-beat clapping rhythm. Each person then presents their own variation on that pattern, which the group claps back to them. This might set up a workshop that explores composing or variations on a theme, and the teaching artist never says one word.

CHECK IN. In a process that's somewhere between a routine and a ritual, many teaching artists will ask to hear something specific from each participant (assuming the numbers are not preclusive) before the work begins. It can be as simple as "a word that captures one feeling you have right now," or it can be more involved—"one sentence about a bright moment in your weekend," or even "a gesture that expresses one feeling about our project." This builds group cohesion, gives the quieter members a speaking moment at the beginning (research shows that this increases their verbal contributions in the activities that follow) and introduces the focus that will unfold over the rest of the workshop.

CHECK OUT OR EXIT TICKET. Honoring the distinctive community that each group becomes, teaching artists often provide a closing ritual as a transition back to "normal" life. Each participant is invited to share one particular thing—perhaps a moment during the workshop they want to remember or an appreciative observation of someone else during the session. Again, everyone makes an offer to the group—everyone, including the quiet one, the one who had a bad moment, the superstar, the one who seemed unhappy—before they go.

When facilitating a regular meeting or a planning session, many teaching artists make "exit tickets" a regular practice in their organizational work: everyone shares an observation about how the meeting went, noting specific things that mattered to them or ways they feel excited or unfinished. This is a reflective practice that builds trust and efficiency over time, and also allows incompletions to be identified so they can be addressed later. Yes, I have introduced this practice within businesses too. It's not touchy-feely—it works.

At the Intersection of Teaching Artistry and Performance

HERE ARE A FEW EXAMPLES of teaching artistry that shapes a new kind of performance.

IN 2002, I worked with the Oregon Symphony as they launched a series of Creative Empowerment Projects. In one, percussionist Chris Perry and violinist Erin Furbee created the "Exploration of Samba and Tango." The audience bought tickets for a 7:00 p.m. performance in a big open space set up with nightclub-like tables, red tablecloths and a rose on each. But the performance didn't begin until 8:00. For that first hour, wine was available and six stations around the periphery of the space invited audience members to visit. There was a section where tango and samba dancing lessons were taught, using music the audience would hear a little later. There was a station with lavish Carnival costumes people could put on for a photo. There was a bandoneon player showing how the instrument worked, letting people try to play it. There was a food station with Brazilian snacks near the bar. Liveliest of all was the percussion zone. An array of hand instruments was spread on a table for anyone to pick up and join an ongoing percussion groove of samba and tango rhythms, following casual prompts from the professionals. In just two minutes, audience members went from awkward fumbling to making Latin music they felt in their bodies. When the concert proper started around 8:00, that audience was primed to love it, to discover things in it. They were having the time of their lives—people spontaneously dancing, tapping rhythms on tables and floor. The performance ended with a samba line that snaked out of the building onto the street, with people grabbing garbage can lids and sticks to keep the rhythmic beat going as they danced together on the street.

David Wallace has written a whole book on interactive concerts, *Engaging the Concert Audience*.[41] If you are curious about this idea, get his excellent book. Here's an example of a concert that Wallace devised. The focus is Stravinsky's six-minute *Elegy for Solo Viola*, written to honor the deceased first violinist Alphonse Onnou of the ProArte Quartet. David begins his event by introducing the subject of grief. He asks the audience to name the range of different feelings that arise in a period of loss. He gets many suggestions, like "periods of numbness" and "hilarious memories" along with various shades of sadness. He asks those who suggested an idea to help him find a way to play something on his viola that captures those particular feelings. He draws people out, trying their ideas, adjusting them; together they find a satisfying sound, a phrase, that fits the specific feeling. After he has done this with several, he says, "There's this phrase from Stravinsky—what feeling does it evoke?" He plays a phrase from the piece, gets answers, and urges them toward greater specificity. Playing the phrase again several times, the answer evolves from the generic "sad" to the poignant "the moment that triggers a big wave of missing." They explore a handful of key phrases from the piece in this way. Then David performs the whole piece. That audience follows it intimately, in empathic connection with each phrase, following its journey, discovering the complexities that Stravinsky was exploring. They co-create the experience of that performance in a way many have never experienced before. The whole activity takes about 25 minutes.

THE TEACHING ARTIST TOM CABANISS, whom I mentioned earlier, designed the first Very Open Rehearsal that I know of. That's not the same as a standard "open rehearsal," in which audiences are allowed to tiptoe in to observe an orchestral rehearsal in progress. The point of an open rehearsal, I guess, is for spectators to be dazzled by the private access to witness creation at work. Unfortunately, they usually can't hear what the conductor is saying to the musicians. And more often than not, the open rehearsal is the final rehearsal, so the creative adjustments are few and subtle.

A Very Open Rehearsal, by contrast, usually has a small ensemble and small audience, and the musicians are really rehearsing, doing the nuts-and-bolts work of getting a piece together. A 75-minute VOR may only focus on a four-minute movement of a string quartet. Its distinctive feature is that audience members can raise a hand and stop the rehearsal to ask a question. The musicians pause to answer as honestly as they can. For example: "You just played that little part four times and were satisfied only with the last one, and I couldn't hear the difference. What was going on?" The musicians describe and demonstrate the technical detail that was so important to them, in a way that, without explanation, the audience would never have understood. I've even heard, "Why do violinists always have hickies on their necks?" The violinist answered, "It's because we hold our violins at the same place under our chins many hours a day, for years. Yeah, it was a real problem in high school." That audience was so much more on the side of that musician after that; she'd become a real person, not just a technical master to admire.

A Very Open Rehearsal usually culminates in a runthrough of the piece they have been working on, and it's common to see a standing ovation afterward—for a four minute piece!—because the audience now grasps the tremendous skill, passion and complexity of their work. They are having flow experiences of total absorption as they listen. I facilitated one VOR in which the quartet was still uncertain about the tempo and overall shape of the final section, so they played it twice, in different ways, and asked the audience to give them feedback on each. It was hard to usher that audience out of the performance space at the end;

they wanted to stay and keep talking. And the musicians wanted to keep talking to audience members who were so completely fascinated by what musicians know and do.

IN THE FARMING TOWN Lambunao, located in The Philippines' Iloilo Province, teaching artist Razcel Jan Salvarita set up a display in the town square. Some 220 terracotta masks were attached to an inverted pyramid-shaped cage, a startling display of faces as part of his "Unmasking Climate Injustices" project. Each had a different expression, designed by local farmers and artisans to share their feelings about the climate crisis' impact on their seasonal farming and lives. They also made a video documentary wherein participants wore their masks and spoke their thoughts behind them. Raz used local clay, local pottery-firing techniques (in the embers of a bonfire) and traditional mask design aesthetics in his workshops. The farmers and artisans learned and discussed the facts of the climate crisis during their work with the clay, and their masks held the anger, sadness, worry and helplessness they felt during the process. They and others were trained as facilitators to lead discussions about the climate issues that were damaging their crop cycles. The town square display was extended by a few months, adding explanatory plaques and having facilitators engage with people in pop-up teach-ins. They used the moment to teach the scientific facts of the climate issues that were so troubling to the region. Since then, the facilitators hold regular instruction sessions about climate issues in a local church; this includes young people who now provide climate education in their school and community. Raz documented the conversations and process so that others can learn from the journey of this community, and then made an online case study[42] others can learn from for free.

The Purple Threads

As good as teaching artists tend to be in action, they tend to be vague in defining what teaching artistry actually is. (As mentioned earlier, this challenge prompted me to lay out the Six Fundamentals.) Well, teaching artists are even hazier in describing the professional field itself. It's not their fault—the field is underdeveloped and complex. The first descriptive schemes described the field by identifying the locations where its members worked. This wasn't helpful because those members were hired to achieve different goals in the same location—for example, in a U.S. school, a teaching artist might be preparing students to see an opera one week and guiding an intergenerational writing project with octogenarians down the hall a week later. Same place, different goals.

> *A good teaching artist works in different settings and takes on different identities based on the project.*

That location-based framework of teaching artistry also encouraged the "silo thinking" that divides and separates the field, weakening it. This makes *teaching artists* seem separate from *community artists* and *social practice artists*. A good teaching artist works in different settings and takes on different identities based on the project. Those titles are no more different than a visual artist working with watercolors one day and collage the next.

In 2011, I published a reframing of the field.[43] As with the Fundamentals, I checked this prototype with many colleagues who have offered a few tweaks over the years. It provided the structure for Lincoln Center's Teaching Artist Development Labs. It isn't perfect, but it clarifies.

This framework highlights the *purposes* for which teaching artists are hired; the goals they design their activities to deliver. Focusing on purpose reduces the false barriers of job titles, as different titles often share the same purpose. The person hired to excite a neighborhood about a new playground may be labeled a teaching artist or a community artist (or a participatory artist in the U.K.)—it doesn't matter. What matters is the process, and the way the neighbors enjoy that park at the end of the project and beyond.

I've defined seven purposes, and I call them threads because they are flexible and often interwoven.

These Purpose Threads are not discrete in actual practice. There is natural overlap. For example, when working to excite the neighborhood about the new playground, a teaching artist is likely to make works of art with that community while also getting neighborhood kids to invent games to play in the open area. Another example of how purposes weave: mezzo-soprano Joyce DiDonato did a world tour of EDEN,[44] her operatic cri-de-coeur for environmentalism. In every city of the tour, a teaching artist in EDEN Engagement[45] (a partnership project with the International Teaching Artist Collaborative, ITAC) worked with a chorus of young people in a low-income neighborhood to creatively explore a local environmental issue, raising their awareness and commitment to change. At the same time, they rehearsed a song they sang in the finale with Joyce on stage in a major opera house; they were rapt in hearing the Handel aria that followed. EDEN Engagement is a weave of Activist, Work of Art, Arts Integration and Personal Development threads.

These threads invite us to ask: What is the main purpose of the project? How would you want the impact of this project to be assessed? So, without further ado, meet the Purpose Threads, listed in no hierarchical order.

1. **Personal Development**
   To develop personal or social capacities.

2. **Community**
   To enhance the life of communities.

3. **Activism**
   To impact a political or social movement.

4. **Partnering for Non-Arts Goals**
   To achieve goals important to other institutions.

5. **Art Skills Development**
   To deepen the development of artmaking skills.

6. **Arts Integration**
   To catalyze the learning of non-arts content.

7. **Work of Art**
   To enrich the encounter with works of art.

1. Personal Development.

PURPOSE: *To develop personal or social capacities.*

EXAMPLE: Brass for Africa[46] works in communities in Uganda, Liberia and Rwanda. Their teachers come from those communities and have the job title "Music and Life Skills Teacher." They are dedicated to modeling the life skills it takes to live an expanded life as they train young musicians who know how to bring their community together in music. Just today I was working with one of their teachers—he was headed for a troubled life before he joined Brass for Africa as a student and later as a teacher, and then as a program leader in the partnership with the Academy for Impact through Music—but that day we were working on his research in the Global Leaders Program about ways that music education can contribute to the United Nations' Sustainable Development Goals.

In this fast-growing body of work, teaching artists or "social practice artists" aim to develop personal or social capacities through creative engagement. These aren't one-shot miracles; humans don't change overnight. Teaching artists work within organizations to achieve social goals over time.

This thread includes the remarkably positive results with people who have disabilities, with people in prison and juvenile detention programs and with students in thousands of after-school programs. It includes the work of creative aging, in which older people make stuff they care about (story theater, dances, choruses, paintings, sculptures, etc.) with measurable benefits like increased longevity, shorter hospital stays, reduced prescription drug intake and less depression. New research is showing promising results with dementia patients as well.

This thread also includes the work of music for social change programs around the world—the hundreds of youth music programs like Brass for Africa that empower young people growing up in the stress of poverty or social upheaval. Many of these programs were inspired by Venezuela's El Sistema. Over years of musical accomplishment with their friends, young musicians make strong positive choices that expand options in their lives; about a million young people around the world are actively involved in such programs today. There are similar programs in dance, theater, visual arts, media arts, hip hop, writing and more. Almost all operate heroically on overstretched budgets.

THE EMERGING INNER DEVELOPMENT GOALS[47] focus on the capacities humans must have if we are to achieve the United Nations' Sustainable Development Goals. Teaching artists know how to deliver those IDGs.

If you were to assess a teaching artist's impact in this thread, you would study the desired personal and social outcomes the programs produce. These outcomes may range from reduced medications to improved morale to health outcomes in senior centers, from reduced recidivism rates to reduced crime involvement to higher graduation rates in music for social change programs.

In terms of assessing the impact of personal/social development programs, this thread shows huge potential for societal improvement. Do you know the term "opportunity cost"? It calculates how an investment in one area can have a financial impact in another area. Basically, it quantifies the value of the road not taken, the sum of what you didn't have to spend. Sistema Scotland[48] is the one music-for-social-change program that has researched the opportunity cost of their work in relation to city social-service expenditures. Independent researchers found that, over time, the cost of the music program was far lower than the social and economic benefits it produced.[49] Within fifteen years, the researchers asserted, Big Noise in Glasgow's Govanhill neighborhood would save the city a total of 29 million pounds in reduced government spending on social welfare, criminal justice and public health. One pound invested in Glasgow teaching artists saves many times that amount in public money. Not many investments can beat that.

2. Community.

PURPOSE: *To enhance the life of communities.*

EXAMPLE: For over thirty years, teaching artists at The Village of Arts and Humanities[50] in North Philadelphia have worked with residents to "amplify the voices and aspirations of our community by providing arts-based opportunities for self-expression and personal success that engage youth and their families, revitalize physical space, and preserve Black heritage." Their newest feature (2023), the Civic Power Studio, aims "to build something the neighborhood never forgets."

In these projects, artists strive to activate and enhance a community's artistic assets in order to enrich its quality of life. The proud, deep traditions of "community artists" and "civic arts practice" inform this thread. Artists serve community needs as they surface, identifying them and then building consensus around addressing those needs. From Theatre for Social Development in Africa, to participatory mural projects in most major cities around the world, to Creative Placemaking projects in the U.S., this work is inherently inclusive—everyone is welcomed, actively recruited and fully engaged. The work goes even better when usually marginalized community members join. There are programs with deep traditions in the U.S., like Appalshop[51] in Appalachia, Cornerstone Theater Company[52] in Los Angeles, Mural Arts Philadelphia[53] and In the Heart of the Beast[54] in Minneapolis, as well as countless projects around the world, like Streetwise Opera[55] in the U.K. Colombian teaching artist Yazmany Arboleda led the Color in Faith[56] project, in which Kenyan communities painted their mosques and churches the same yellow, with faithful members of both religions working together to affirm local harmony. Yazmany now works as the Artist-in-Residence in New York City's Civic Engagement Commission.

If you were to assess a teaching artist's work in this thread, you would look at the impact on community members, how their attitudes and behaviors change and perhaps even how the community's functioning has changed.

3. Activism.

PURPOSE: *To impact a political or social movement.*

THREE EXAMPLES: 1) At ITAC6 (The Sixth International Teaching Artist Conference, 2022) in Oslo, a group of 20 teaching artists, with skin, hair and clothes painted gray, moved slowly through downtown Oslo, pausing occasionally in somber tableaux, before ending up in front of the Parliament building. To the hundreds who stopped to look, including elected officials, they handed out small slips of paper with the facts about the 1.2

billion climate refugees the world will see by 2050 if we don't keep to 1.5 degrees of temperature rise.

2) The field of ARTIVISM is rising, with dedicated but isolated individual artists and programs around the world beginning to come together and make beautiful trouble. For almost thirty years, Big hART in Australia[57] (among other creative youth development programs around the world) has worked with young people (over 8,000) in fifty-two "communities of need" to develop artworks and artists who directly address social challenges.

3) "CRAFTIVISM: Changing the world one stitch at a time,"[58] was devised by founding teaching artist Sarah Corbett in England. She calls it political activism for introverts. Small groups gather to craft beautiful works with ingenious and sometimes devious intent—like the lovely pillow, needlepointed with subversive political messages, that ended up on a Prime Minister's sofa.

WHEN A COMMUNITY RISES to change what's unacceptable, activism begins. Teaching artists can make a difference, whether in a small community that demands a shared garden on a vacant plot of land or in a large community that demands social, racial or gender justice. Teaching artists have a long history of engaging participants to change minds, challenge ideas, build solidarity and revise the status quo. This work often intends to be provocative, even disturbing; sometimes it is labeled "propaganda." It includes Theater of the Oppressed, street theater, songs, graffiti and public artworks. Think Banksy; think Olafur Eliasson, who placed large blocks of Arctic ice in major city squares where they would publicly, poignantly melt.

> When a community rises to change what's unacceptable, activism begins.

This thread appears around the world in the artworks that carry messages of protest and outrage, and in the teaching artists who use their skills to creatively engage and challenge others. My friend Chen Alon co-founded Combatants for Peace in Israel, in which Israeli and Palestinian actors work as peacemakers (he was nominated for the Nobel Peace Prize). The Afghanistan National Institute of Music (ANIM) was founded by Dr. Ahmad Sarmast with the goal of restoring a national music industry after it had been eliminated by the Mujahideen and Taliban. At ANIM, women were trained as full equals by the teaching artists; all the young musicians embraced the organization's social responsibility until forced to escape into exile when the Taliban regained control in 2021. Sarmast was also nominated for the Nobel Peace Prize.

Whole artistic genres have been born out of activist movements, such as the Nigerian rock music movement of the 1960s or krumping (a dance form born in Los Angeles) in the 1990s. Some argue that hip-hop arose from a political imperative. In the street theater anti-war protests of my youth, we didn't just "put on a show" in public spaces, we engaged with the audiences to draw them in as participants, grappling with the political conflicts in the performance. Playback Theatre[59] (now active around the world) uses its illuminating theatrical insight to elevate the personal stories of people impacted by injustice or social challenge.

> *Whole artistic genres have been born out of activist movements*

If you were to assess the artist-activist's work in this thread, you would try to determine the lingering effect in people's hearts, minds and actions.

4. **Partnering for Non-Arts Goals.**

PURPOSE: *To achieve goals important to other institutions.*

TWO EXAMPLES: 1) A teaching-artist-in-residence[60] works with project teams in New York City's Sanitation Department to think more creatively about solving the perennial communication difficulties around changes in garbage pickups.

2) Clowns Without Borders[61] began in 1993, when children in Barcelona raised funds to send a famous clown to refugee camps in Croatia; they got the idea from their refugee pen pals, who said, "We miss laughter." Now, with chapters in fifteen countries, CWB works with local aid agencies in 123 countries to address trauma with humor in crisis situations.

Teaching artists and visionary organizations are experimenting widely in this growing area. Yes, this thread has a dull title, but the range of experimentation within it is anything but dull. The field of play is so broad that I don't know how else to title it. This thread finds teaching artists working with businesses to increase innovation, to build teamwork, to boost creativity and to develop leadership skills. Teaching artists work with medical schools and hospitals to increase diagnostic acuity and to deepen empathy, which improves the emotional component of their work and reduces suffering. They work with planning commissions to bring creative vitality to urban planning. New York City's PAIR program (Public Artists in Residence, cited above) has placed artists in eleven government agencies to help them overcome long-term weaknesses in fulfilling their mandates; Los Angeles and at least a dozen other U.S. cities have some version of this too. The fields of Impact Investing and Social Impact Bonds are discovering the power of teaching artists—such initiatives actually earn a financial return for investors on the measurable positive impact of projects. I often say, "Invest in teaching artists," and in this thread, it gets literal.

Teaching artistry as a field has not investigated this thread yet; it pops up unpredictably as various organizations discover ways that creative engagement can help them achieve their objectives. The teaching artist field doesn't communicate well about the opportunities, practices or successes to build upon—just yesterday I stumbled on a report[62] detailing a dozen ways teaching artists are involved in U.S. transportation infrastructure projects. How very smart it would be for a funder to bring together teaching artists who have served in projects like these, to learn from their experience (not always positive) and advance the professional learning in this thread.

To assess the teaching artist's work in this thread, you would focus on the goals of the specific project and find out if they are being attained. I didn't know if my work on creative processes with a group of high-tech metallurgical engineers working on surgical products had a measurable impact until I got a short thank-you note two years later, describing a new kind of stent they had just produced and mentioning the fun they were having in experimenting with ways to improve golf clubs.

5. **ART SKILLS DEVELOPMENT.**
   PURPOSE: *To deepen and widen the development of artmaking skills.*

   EXAMPLE: The Longy School of Music of Bard College in Cambridge, Massachusetts, is the conservatory most advanced in the belief that music skills must be blended with teaching artist skills to develop successful, responsible, creatively fulfilled 21st-century musicians. Students must take a series of courses and develop a community project to graduate. Longy's faculty is trained to teach and coach like teaching artists so that they model the school's commitment. Longy even published *The Ensemble*[63] for a time—the largest publication for the global music for social change movement, whose workforce is teaching artists.

Teaching artistry has a place in the training of artists. Because tunnel-focused, technical, mechanical and mimetic learning still dominates much artist training, teaching artistry becomes important for broadening and deepening individual artistry. Arts teaching aspires to produce professionalism within a particular art form; teaching artistry aspires to produce people who are artistically alive. There is no clear dividing line between teaching artists and arts teachers. Arts teachers who prioritize artistic breadth and creative aliveness in their emerging artists, and model it in the way they teach, *are* teaching artists. The inverse is true too—if teaching artists are given enough time with students, they love to advance technique because it inspires both commitment to the art form and better artists. The suffusion of teaching artistry into the training of artists is, to me, a major part of the solution to the high arts' long-term problems. Let's train the next generation of artists to be as eager to engage audiences about the processes and verbs of their art as they do about the culminating nouns they must pay to come see.

Artist-training institutions are beginning to recognize that teaching artistry has something powerful to bring to the development of artists. We discovered this at Juilliard, where I co-founded and led the teaching artist program: those who became adept teaching artists in their Juilliard graduate school years rarely followed the tunnel track into orchestral careers. Instead, they created unusually varied careers in which they retained artistic control that allowed them to make innovative contributions to the field—and to have higher incomes on average. In these pages, I have repeatedly cited the visionary programs of Carnegie Hall's education department, which have been created and led by Sarah Johnson, a graduate of that Juilliard teaching artist program.

Other examples: Teaching artists at Say Sí[64] in San Antonio develop young artists in many disciplines, but those young artists are not just career-focused actors and filmmakers; they are community-minded contributors through their art. The teaching artists at Marwen,[65] in Chicago, nurture professional-level accomplishment in their young visual artists in such a way that positive life change is a consistent side-effect of their learning.

If you were to assess the teaching artist's work in this thread, you would seek to assess the motivation of the learner, the development of individual voice and the strength of the personally relevant connections the learner makes inside and outside of the discipline.

6. Arts Integration.

PURPOSE: *To catalyze the learning of non-arts content.*

EXAMPLE: In a Finnish high school English language classroom I visited, a teaching artist/sound designer was working with students on a podcast project called This Finnish Life, based on the U.S. podcast *This American Life*. The students were polishing their English throughout the writing, editing and production processes. When I was there, the teaching artist and students were putting the finishing touches, including exact grammar, improved pronunciation and just the right idioms, on their segment "The Best Pickup Lines in Finnish Bars." They told me, in detailed English, how much they enjoyed their research interviews.

Arts integration brings arts learning together with other subject material so that both advance further and delve deeper than they would on their own. This is the largest experiment happening in U.S. arts education. It's risky too. We could end up with the arts serving as handmaidens to the "serious" subjects that schools care more about—the arts used merely to pep up a boring curriculum in history, science or math. I've seen it happen. I saw the "Dance of the Fractions," in which kids presented a movement sequence, set to pop music, that demonstrated fraction-relationships. It was charming. And accurate.

Significantly, those students tested better in that section of their math studies, allowing that school to brag about its successful "dance-integrated *math curriculum*."

The problem was that exactly no arts learning was happening. It was a perfectly good kinesthetic math project—nothing wrong with that, for sure—but don't mistake it for arts-integrated learning, because the kids learned nothing about dance, made no choices based on dance ideas and were no more interested in dance at the end. The arts actually lost ground in that school—who is going to challenge a fun body-math curriculum to focus more on dance when the curriculum reliably raises test scores as it is? I've also seen the opposite imbalance, where a core subject is used as an excuse to do a cool arts project. Like the Rainforest Rag composition project, in which nature sounds were included in the lively and complex score with invented notation that covered a classroom wall. That process didn't excite any extra interest in the ways rainforests work.

Arts integration can be a hard balancing act because one focus can easily dominate the other. To succeed, the teaching artist and partner teacher must both feel that the learning they care about most is advancing through the work and beyond the project. A great example is the arts-integrated project that teaching artist Evan Premo led with biology and music students in Vermont. The students worked together to meticulously and musically capture the ways the human body fights infections. They composed the three-movement *ImmunoSymphony*—the cytotoxic T cells got the heroic theme. The culminating movement, entitled "The Rusty Nail," had the tam tam announce the puncture, and "a string player doing a half step trill with a molto crescendo leading to an accented fortississimo eighth note" represent the theme of the T cells at work. Spoiler alert: the body wins.

There are hundreds of programs and experiments of this kind across the U.S. They go by many names, including STEM to STEAM (science-technology-engineering-math becoming science-technology-engineering-arts-math), arts project-based learning and arts-rich and arts-infused curriculum. The Leonard Bernstein Foundation's network of Artful Learning[66] schools work deeply in this thread, as do many charter schools[67] and some programs of Young Audiences and The Kennedy Center. The thread is not limited to the U.S.; I have helped schools in seven countries adopt arts-integrated curricula. Finland uses this approach widely and has the highest academic achievement record in the world (their PISA ranking moves among the top three from year to year).

If you were assessing the teaching artist's work in this thread, you would be interested in the specific learning and the intrinsic motivation developed in both the particular art form and the particular subject area. For example, in a theater and history project, you might assess what students learned about writing strong scenes as well as what they learned about that scene's historical context.

7. Work of Art.

PURPOSE: *To enrich the encounter with works of art.*

EXAMPLE: Carnegie Hall's Link Up[68] program asked, "If a student were able to attend only one live orchestral concert, what are all the things we could do to maximize the impact of that experience?" Their teaching artists designed a flexible curriculum, a series of activities and culminating performances that are now used by over 100 orchestras around the world.

The core goal in this thread is to support people's capacity to make meaningful connections inside the artworks they encounter. When it comes down to the crucial one-on-one moment—this person and this artwork—can the individual audience member get inside and discover things that are valuable to them? Remember my working definition of the artistic experience: making personally relevant connections outside of what one already knows. This is the goal of "outreach"[69] in most arts organizations—to introduce, excite and engage people in their art offerings.

This purpose was the first identity of teaching artistry in the U.S., at Lincoln Center in the 1970s and increasingly as teaching artists were hired in the early 1980s to go into schools in response to the arts education cutbacks of the Ronald Reagan administration. Arts advocates feared that a generation of young Americans would grow up with no feel for the high arts. (This fear has proven real.) This Purpose Thread was the core of Leonard Bernstein's Young People's Concerts, the aim of Young Audiences (the largest and oldest network in the U.S. that employs teaching artists) and the goal of Visual Thinking Strategies, a practice so influential in the museum world. Teaching artists often accomplish this goal by having participants make works of art that run parallel to what the artist was working on. When I was preparing teenagers to see *Hamlet*, we started with their creating soliloquies about a moral issue that mattered to them.

If you were to assess a teaching artist's work in this thread, you would look into the quality of one's engagement with the artworks and the impact of those encounters.

*

SO THAT'S THE WEAVE of the global teaching artist workforce. When I share this framework with teaching artists, it's usually a discovery for them to see the seven threads laid out with clarity. Together, we consider what it's like to work in threads they haven't tried. This leads to a discussion about the skills, practices and ways of thinking that are universal across all threads, and those that are particular to different threads and traditions. That leads right into endlessly fascinating discussions about the best ways to train teaching artists. But that's the focus of a different book.

Or maybe not a book? ITAC recently launched its first online course, called "Teaching Artistry for Social Impact."[70] (It lives on the Kadenze platform.[71]) A teaching artist who takes that course might use it to prepare for projects in different Purpose Threads—maybe for Activism or Partnering for Non-Arts Goals, or even Personal Development. Each student in the course crafts a personal passion project throughout the course, applying all the features of the curriculum to their own vision, identifying which thread is being pursued and detailing ways to document the *impact*.

Beyond a Specific Purpose

The best things in life are the things that can't be named; the second best things in life are the things that refer to the best things in life; and the third best things are what we talk about.
—JOSEPH CAMPBELL

ORGANIZATIONAL CHART ARROWS don't point to the best things in life. As helpfully true as the Fundamentals and Purposes Threads of teaching artistry may be, they aren't the reason so many thousands of teaching artists fall in love with the work and spend a lifetime with it, in spite of its difficulties. The inner life of teaching artistry provides the sustaining wealth that professional life can only partly provide.

*

THE FINAL DAY of ITAC6 (the Sixth International Teaching Artist Conference, 2022) in Oslo began with a dance performance by a teaching artist dance ensemble from South Korea. Their government agency KACES[72] had hosted ITAC5, and this dance premiere celebrated a research project KACES led after ITAC5 about teaching artistry in their country. The study's key finding was how powerful it was for individual teaching artists to feel that they are a part of a community of practice. They'd made a film of eloquent statements by Korean teaching artists that the dancers initially lip-synched, and then spoke, before they evolved into movement. Movement that made K-pop look lackadaisical. The dance was ingenious in sharing the inner life of teaching artistry—the hundreds of teaching artists in the room from 28 countries and all art forms, and hundreds more connected via livestream from a dozen additional countries, recognized themselves in the dance. They were seeing their identity embodied for the first time.

Just when I thought the dance was coming to a climax, it made a teaching artist move to burst off the stage and into the audience. Dancers activated seated audience members to join them, improvising with the movement themes they had introduced. The momentum built until the audience had disrupted the careful rows of chairs we started in and an organic whole-group dance had emerged—teaching artistry in sweaty action. The dancers didn't end it; the community did. They knew when it was over and announced it with an ecstatic cheer. This was a community that had found itself. After millennia of making contributions, centuries of visible practice, decades of professional growth and years of building a first network of connection, teaching artistry had found its identity. As I said, the etymology of *identity* means the *same*.

I LOVE MOVING through the world as an artist. When I set aside the relentless thinking and planning and relax into my artist self, I see and hear things I otherwise miss. I sense and discover patterns, little surprises, ironies and beauty that usually abides unnoticed. I get unexpected ideas, some of which are worth hanging out with, among the usual mental bric-a-brac. This quality of experiencing daily life is one of the secret benefits of a life as an artist. Don't tell anyone; it sounds artsy-fluffy. Unless you have experienced it.

I love moving through the world as a teaching artist even more. Just as teaching artistry is an expansion of being an artist, I get all those artist benefits, plus more. My teaching artist spirit adds a layer of interconnectedness to other people and to the things people make—whether they know it or not. I can sense the creative potential in people, knowing it is right there, under the surface, even in the stressed bank teller who clearly hates her job but does this playful little dance with her museum-quality fingernails as she hands me a receipt. It's on the surface too, in the stories people tell when they switch into true telling and not just repeating or showing off. I can see their artistry in action. It's there in the things they create, like that vegetable pie my wife improvised last week. Imagine moving through the world seeing creative potential everywhere, just under the surface, hoping to be activated, shyly reaching out. It's alive and eager to be liberated from the control panel of assumptions, opinions, judgments and necessity. This is the home base of social imagination, where we are radically connected and brimming with possibility. (The etymology of *radical* means *connected at the roots*.) It isn't self-absorbed. It's way more fun. It serves. Teaching artistry serves me as well as others I come in contact with. It is my everyday way to—remembering that sixth Fundamental—reach beyond the literal, beyond the "good enough," beyond right answers, standard solutions, existing opinions and judgments, to see the world as if it could be otherwise. It's a way to bring that new world into being.

*

AS IF FROM CENTRAL CASTING, his name was Buck, a man of few words and a lot of horsepower. He was deft with his diesel pickup and plow—a good thing, because my first winter after moving to the countryside had more snow than anyone had seen in years. One snowfall was particularly challenging for Buck, forcing him to push back the existing banks of snow, already so high, before he could plow up the fresh ten inches. My driveway is quirky, curved and enforced by big trees; it flummoxes everyone who tries to back out. Anxiously, I watched the lurching and zooming, the metal racket of the plow in the snowy quiet, thinking, "Buck, be careful of the trees." He came inches from gouging them but never touched a single one. It took him most of an hour to complete what normally takes ten minutes.

When Buck finished plowing, he paused at the end of the driveway and just sat for a time. He had many more driveways to plow, but he seemed to like this spot. I imagine he was reflecting on things, taking in the beauty after spending all that time pushing it around. This time, I walked to the truck to talk to him in his reverie. It was after midnight. He rolled down the window but kept looking straight ahead. "Buck, I watched the whole thing. That was really amazing. You did an incredible job." Still for a few moments, without turning toward me, he finally nodded, "It was a work of art." Just that. That said it all.

* * *

Acknowledgements

THERE ARE too many to thank for making the decades of my freelance teaching artist career possible. So many projects, so many great people, so many inspiring colleagues—if you are thinking I might mean *you*, I do. The thanks for this short book go to a shorter list.

Thanks to those whose direct help made all the difference. Most of all to my wife Tricia Tunstall, who is conveniently a great teaching artist, a better writer than I am and a superb editor. And boundlessly generous on top of that. Thanks to my sister Amy Miller who writes elegantly and reads insightfully, and who gave excellent feedback on emerging drafts. Thanks also to the skilled colleagues whose expertise brought this book to the finish line: editor Patrick Scafidi and designer Tilman Reitzle. And thanks to Brian Horner and Paul Gamble, who carried this book into the world.

I am always grateful to my close colleagues who keep inspiring and encouraging me: the team at the International Teaching Artist Collaborative (especially Managing Director and Universal Hero Madeleine McGirk and Chairman Yonglun Liu) and our colleagues at the Community Arts Network (Anis Barnat, Samar Bandak, Christina Desinioti and Werner Binnenstein-Bachstein). Thanks to the Leonard Bernstein Foundation and the Fertel Foundation for support in getting this book into many readers' hands.

About the Author

A PRACTICING teaching artist for forty-four years, working with the world's most prestigious organizations (including Lincoln Center, Carnegie Hall, The Kennedy Center, Juilliard, seven of the ten largest orchestras in the U.S. and organizations in sixteen other countries) and hundreds of grassroots initiatives, Eric Booth is widely called "the father of the teaching artist profession." A Broadway actor, successful entrepreneur, keynote speaker, global consultant and teacher, and author of seven previous books, he co-founded the

International Teaching Artist Collaborative (ITAC), the first global network of artists who work in communities and schools. He lives in Hudson River Valley north of New York City, and works actively with programs around the world, especially Vermont's Community Engagement Lab, the Academy for Impact through Music and the Global Leaders Institute. His website is: ericbooth.net

About ITAC

THE INTERNATIONAL Teaching Artist Collaborative (ITAC) is the first global network of artists who work in communities and schools. Founded in 2012 (by Eric Booth and Marit Ulvund of Norway's SEANSE[73]) with the first International Teaching Artist Conference, in Oslo, ITAC has held biennial global gatherings in Brisbane, Edinburgh, New York (at Carnegie Hall), Seoul (held virtually because of the Covid pandemic), Oslo (again to celebrate its first decade) and in New Zealand in 2024. Becoming a year-round organization in 2018, ITAC has connected thousands of members and dozens of projects, commissioning projects on every continent (except Antarctica—still hoping!). Working groups of teaching artists are building new resources for the field, and an active Climate Collective pioneers teaching artistry that addresses the climate crisis. Membership is free: https://www.itac-collaborative.com/get-involved/donate

I HOPE THIS BOOK has moved you to support teaching artists globally and locally. You can always make a donation through the ITAC website (follow the QR code on this page) or donate locally to support a teaching artist organization near you.

If you would like to distribute copies of this book to help a particular program or to advocate for teaching artistry in general, please go to the book's website (www.teachingartistsmakingchange.com) to find out how. We need and welcome your help.

Endnotes

1. https://www.artolution.org
2. https://dreamorchestra.se
3. https://www.platocultural.com
4. https://www.itac-collaborative.com
5. https://sdgs.un.org/goals
6. https://www.innerdevelopmentgoals.org
7. Walter Benjamin, The Work of Art in the Age of Mechanical Reproduction (London: Penguin, 2008).
8. https://www.wallacefoundation.org/knowledge-center/pages/gifts-of-the-muse.aspx
9. https://www.thersa.org/reports/arts-cultural-schools
10. https://turnaroundarts.kennedy-center.org
11. https://www.leonardbernstein.com/artful-learning
12. https://www.shakespeare.org/education/shakespeare-in-the-courts
13. http://www.sistemawhangarei.org.nz
14. https://dreamorchestra.se
15. https://elsistema.gr
16. https://www.soundsofchange.org
17. https://teachingartists.com
18. https://www.artworksalliance.org.uk
19. https://www.aimpowers.com
20. Aesthetic Perspectives from Animating Democracy identifies these and eight other kinds of excellence that teaching artists find in community arts projects: https://www.animatingdemocracy.org/aesthetic-perspectives
21. A question devised by teaching artist David Wallace in his school residency within Juilliard's Morse Fellowship Program
22. https://www.carnegiehall.org/Education/Programs/Lullaby-Project
23. https://soundcloud.com/carnegiehalllullaby
24. https://www.ariveroflightinwaterbury.org
25. https://ariveroflight.org/about
26. https://www.epictheatreensemble.org/learn/shakespeare-remix
27. https://en.dahteatarcentar.com/performances/dancing-trees. Also here: https://www.itac-collaborative.com/projects/teaching-artistry-for-social-impact-case-studies
28. https://www.communityengagementlab.org
29. https://www.musicianswithoutborders.org
30. https://usdac.us/artisticresponse
31. https://usdac.us
32. https://artistyear.org
33. https://cfpeace.org/about
34. https://www.norc.org/Research/Projects/Pages/Teaching-Artists-Research-Project-TARP.aspx
35. https://www.artworksalliance.org.uk/knowledge-bank

36 https://www.itac-collaborative.com/projects/teaching-artistry-for-social-impact
37 https://elsistema.org.ve
38 https://vtshome.org/
39 https://www.artspractica.com/about
40 http://ericbooth.net/reflecting-on-reflection
41 https://www.amazon.com/Engaging-Concert-Audience-Interactive-Performance/dp/0876391919
42 https://www.kadenze.com/courses/climate-case-studies/sessions/unmasking-climate-injustices-in-the-philippines
43 http://ericbooth.net/857-2
44 https://eden.joycedidonato.com
45 https://www.itac-collaborative.com/projects/eden-engagement
46 https://www.brassforafrica.org
47 https://www.innerdevelopmentgoals.org
48 https://www.makeabignoise.org.uk/sistema-scotland
49 https://www.makeabignoise.org.uk/research, especially this study: https://www.makeabignoise.org.uk/research/glasgow-centre-population-health
50 https://spaces.villagearts.org
51 https://appalshop.org/story
52 https://cornerstonetheater.org
53 https://www.muralarts.org
54 https://hobt.org
55 https://streetwiseopera.org
56 https://www.colourinfaith.com
57 https://www.bighart.org/
58 https://craftivist-collective.com
59 https://playbacknorthamerica.com/about/playback-2
60 The PAIR Program/Public Artists in Residence; https://www.nyc.gov/site/dcla/publicart/pair.page
61 https://clownswithoutborders.org
62 https://nasaa-arts.org/nasaa_research/arts-in-transportation-strategy-sampler
63 https://ensemblenews.org
64 https://saysi.org
65 https://marwen.org
66 https://www.leonardbernstein.com/artful-learning/schools
67 I recommend readers learn about the exemplary work at the Renaissance Arts Academy in Los Angeles, which is arts-rich and among the highest achieving public schools in the area. https://www.renarts.org
68 https://www.carnegiehall.org/Education/Programs/Link-Up
69 The term "outreach" has fallen into disfavor because of its disrespect for the cultural wealth of those it hopes to reach. The terms "community relations" or "engagement" are now more common.
70 https://www.itac-collaborative.com/projects/teaching-artistry-for-social-impact
71 https://www.kadenze.com/courses/teaching-artistry-for-social-impact/info
72 Korea Arts Culture Education Service: http://eng.arte.or.kr
73 Norway's Seanse Art Center: https://seanse.no/en

Other Books on Teaching Artistry

The Everyday Work of Art, Eric Booth, 1997

The Music Teaching Artists Bible, Eric Booth, 2009

Aesthetics of Generosity: El Sistema, Music Education, and Social Change, Jose Luis Hernandez Estrada, 2012

The Reflexive Teaching Artist, Daniel A. Kelin II and Kathryn Dawson, 2014

Teaching Artist's Handbook Volume One: Tools, Techniques, and Ideas to Help Any Artist Teach, Nick Jaffe, Becca Barniskas, and Barbara Hackett, 2015

A Teaching Artists Companion, Daniel Levy, 2019

Index

A

Abreu, José Antonio 57
Activism 87, 90, 100
Afghanistan 7, 92
Afghanistan National Institute of Music 92
AI. *See* artificial intelligence
AIDS/HIV pandemic 15
AIM (Academy for Impact through Music) 30, 79, 87, 106
Albania 7
Alon, Chen 92
ANIM. *See* Afghanistan National Institute of Music
Appalshop 90
Arboleda, Yazmany 90
A River of Light 41
Art Became the Oxygen 52
Artful Learning 20, 98
artificial intelligence 26
artistry 11–16, 18–33, 35–36, 38, 40, 42, 45, 46, 48, 52, 53, 61–64, 67, 70–72, 81, 85, 94, 95, 99, 101–103, 106–108
ArtistYear 54
Artivism 91
Artolution 7
arts for social impact 12
Arts Integration 86, 87, 96
Art Skills Development 87, 94
arts vocabulary 22, 72
ArtWorks Alliance 30, 55
assessment 46, 70, 74, 75

B

Banksy 91
Belgrade, Serbia 42
Benjamin, Walter 16
Big hART 91
Big Noise 89
Bohm, David 18
Brahms, Johannes 18
Brass for Africa 87, 88
Bravo policy 77
Broadway 42, 43, 44, 105
Burning Man 53

C

Cabaniss, Thomas 40, 71, 82
Campbell, Joseph 101
Carnegie Hall 7, 24, 40, 95, 98, 105, 106
cave paintings 12
Chicago, IL 96
Children's Defense Fund 52
Civic Engagement Commission 90
Civic Power Studio 89. *See also* Village of Arts and Humanities

climate crisis 14, 22, 65, 84, 106
Clowns Without Borders 93
collective artmaking 14
Colombia 19
Color in Faith 90
Combatants for Peace 54, 92
Community Engagement Lab 51
competence 11, 35, 38, 71, 72, 73
Corbett, Sarah 91
Cornerstone Theater Company 90
Costa, Arthur 65
Covid pandemic 32, 106
Craftivism 91
Creative Placemaking 90
creativity coaches 50
Creativity Corps 54
criminal justice 53, 89
Croatia 93
Cunningham, Merce 53
CWB. *See* Clowns Without Borders

D

Dah Theater 42
Dancing Trees 42
detention 20, 88
Dewey, John 73
DiDonato, Joyce 86
disabilities 32, 56, 88
  people with 32
Douglass, Frederick 17
Dream Orchestra 8, 21, 51
Duchamp, Marcel 75

E

Eagen, Emily 40
EDEN Engagement 86
Elegy for Solo Viola 82
Eliasson, Olafur 91
Ellington, Duke 7
El Sistema 21, 57, 88, 89, 109
  Greece 21
  Scotland 89
  Venezuela 57
enabling constraints 71
engagement before information 64

Engaging the Concert Audience 82
Epic Theatre Ensemble 41
exit ticket 79
extrinsic motivation 37

F

Federal Express leadership program 26
Finland 51, 96, 98
fundamentals 5, 45, 85, 101
Furbee, Erin 81

G

GIA (Grantmakers in the Arts) 48
Gothenburg, Sweden 7
Great Depression 28
Greene, Maxine 29, 35, 42

H

Hamlet 41, 99
Heart of the Beast 90
Her Majesty's Education Inspectorate 70
Housen, Abigail 66

I

ImmunoSymphony 97
Impact Investing 93
Indianapolis, IN 38
International Rescue Committee 52
intrinsic motivation 37
Israel 92
ITAC (International Teaching Artist Collaborative) 2, 14, 23, 30, 56, 86, 100, 105, 106

J

Jacobi Medical Center 40
Johnson, Sarah 95
Juilliard School 95, 105, 107

K

KACES 101
Kennedy Center 98, 105
krumping 92

L

Lambunao, Philippines 84
Law of 80% 46, 63
Leonard Bernstein Foundation 98, 105
Liberia 87
Lincoln Center 28, 42, 45, 85, 99, 105
Link Up 98
Los Angeles 90, 92, 93, 108
Lullaby Project, The 40, 50, 71

M

Marwen 96
Miller, Alexa 66
Minneapolis, MN 90
mistake of the day 78
Mozart, Wolfgang Amadeus 67, 68, 69
Mt. Sinai Hospital 26
Mural Arts Philadelphia 90
Museum of Modern Art 66
museums 16, 72, 99, 102

N

New Deal 28, 54
New York City 28, 41, 90, 93, 106
New Zealand 20, 106
Nigeria 92
Nobel Peace Prize 92
non-governmental organizations 14
North Philadelphia 89

O

observation before interpretation 65
Onnou, Alphonse 82
Oregon Symphony 81
Oslo, Norway 90, 101, 106

P

PAIR. *See* Public Artists in Residence
Paleolithic Era 28
Palestinian 54, 92
Partnering for Non-Arts Goals 87, 93, 100
Peace Corps 54
Perry, Chris 81
Personal Development 86, 87, 100
personal relevance 37, 38, 65
Picasso, Pablo 25, 75
Platô Cultural 8
Playback Theatre 92
Premo, Evan 97
ProArte Quartet 82
Public Artists in Residence 93, 108
Purpose Threads 6, 85, 86, 100

R

Reagan administration 99
Red Crescent 52
Red Cross 52
reflection 73
refugees 7, 91
River of Light 41
Rohingya Refugee Camp 7
Rwanda 87

S

Salvarita, Razcel Jan 84
Samba 81
San Antonio, TX 95
Savoor, Gowri 41
Say Sí 95
scaffolding 67
School of the (Im)Possible, The 8
Schubart, Mark 28, 29
Scotland 8, 70, 89
SEANSE 106
self-assessment 46, 74
set up and shut up 63
Shakespeare & Company 20
Shaw, George Bernard 61
Shostakovich, Dmitri 25
Sing Sing Correctional Facility 7
slow down to speed up 37, 38
Social Impact Bonds 93
South Bronx 42
South Korea 101
STEAM 15, 98
STEM 15, 98
St. Louis, MO 48
Stravinsky, Igor 82

Streetwise Opera 90
Sweden 7, 21, 51

T

Taming of the Shrew, The 69
Tango 81
tap competence 71
Teaching Artist Development Labs 45, 85
Teaching Artist Guild 30
Theatre for Social Development in Africa 90
The Everyday Work of Art 25, 109
The Longy School of Music of Bard College 94
thermodynamics
    first law of 27
Tunstall, Tricia 58, 105
Turnaround Arts 20

U

Uganda 87
U.K. 21, 29, 30, 31, 50, 55, 86, 90
Ulvund, Marit 106
United Nations 15, 52, 54, 58, 87, 88
United Nations' Sustainable Development Goals 15, 58, 87, 88
U.S. Department of Arts and Culture 52

V

Venezuela 88
Vermont, USA 41, 51, 97, 106
Very Open Rehearsal 82, 83
Village of Arts and Humanities, The 89
visual artists 53, 96
VTS (Visual Thinking Strategies) 66, 99

W

Wallace, David 82, 107
Wallace Foundation, The 17
warm-up 78
Waterbury, VT 41
Works Progress Administration 28, 54
World Bank 52, 58
World Health Organization 52
WPA. *See* Works Progress Administration

Y

Yenawine, Philip 66
Young Audiences 28, 98, 99
Young People's Concerts 99

Printed by Amazon Italia Logistica S.r.l.
Torrazza Piemonte (TO), Italy